Art
to wear

Jana Ewy

NORTH LIGHT BOOKS
CINCINNATI, OHIO
www.artistsnetwork.com

About the Author

JANA EWY is a talented author, designer, demonstrator and product developer. She is a member of the Society of Craft Designers and often contributes project ideas to popular craft magazines, such as *Teddy Crafts* and *Craftworks*. She also frequently appears as a guest on television shows such as the *Carol Duvall Show* and the Do It Yourself Network's jewelry-making series to demonstrate a wide range of crafting techniques.

Art to Wear. Copyright © 2005 by Jana Ewy. Manufactured in The United States of America. All rights reserved. The patterns and drawings in this book are for personal use of the crafter. By permission of the author and publisher, they may be hand-traced or photocopied to make single copies, but may not be resold or republished under any circumstances. No other part of this book may be reproduced in any form or by any electronic or mechanical means including information storage and retrieval systems without permission in writing from the publisher, except by a reviewer who may quote brief passages in a review. Published by North Light Books, an imprint of F+W Publications, Inc., 4700 East Galbraith Road, Cincinnati, Ohio 45236. (800) 289-0963. First Edition.

Other fine North Light Books are available from your local bookstore, art supply store or direct from the publisher.

09   08   07   06   5   4   3   2

Library of Congress Cataloging-in-Publication Data
Ewy, Jana
    Art to wear/Jana Ewy.
        p. cm.
    Includes index.
    ISBN-13: 978-1-58180-597-0 (pbk. : alk. paper)
    ISBN-10: 1-58180-597-7 (pbk. : alk. paper)
    1. Dressmaking. 2. Jewelry. I. Title.
TT515.E89 2005
646.4'04—dc22

Editors: Jenny Fellinger, Jessica Gordon
Designer: Stephanie Strang
Layout Artist: Kathy Gardner
Production Coordinator: Robin Richie
Photographers: Tim Grondin and Hal Barkan

F+W PUBLICATIONS, INC.

metric conversion chart

TO CONVERT	TO	MULTIPLY BY
Inches	Centimeters	2.54
Centimeters	Inches	0.4
Feet	Centimeters	30.5
Centimeters	Feet	0.03
Yards	Meters	0.9
Meters	Yards	1.1
Sq. Inches	Sq. Centimeters	6.45
Sq. Centimeters	Sq. Inches	0.16
Sq. Feet	Sq. Meters	0.09
Sq. Meters	Sq. Feet	10.8
Sq. Yards	Sq. Meters	0.8
Sq. Meters	Sq. Yards	1.2
Pounds	Kilograms	0.45
Kilograms	Pounds	2.2
Ounces	Grams	28.4
Grams	Ounces	0.04

Dedication*

*This book is dedicated to my mom,

who has been my creative inspiration throughout my life. As a child, I remember watching her sewing, painting or drawing, and it was with her encouragement that I embarked on my own creative journey. As an adult, I am continuing that journey with each new project I dream up and with each new book I write. In passing on her artistic spirit and her love of crafting to me, my mother has given me an incredible gift. She has been there with me along every twist and turn of my designing path—maybe she's not always glad to be along for the ride, but she's there nonetheless. This book is no exception. Once again my mom came when I called, and together we worked on several of the projects that fill these pages. Thanks, Mom, for your creative spirit and for always being there when I need you. I love you!

*Many thanks to my family and friends, who have always given me such wonderful support, encouragement and inspiration. Thank you as well to the many manufacturers who have given so generously of their wonderful products. I would also like to thank the staff at North Light Books, whose warmth and kindness made the process of writing this book a pure pleasure. You have my admiration for producing such a quality product.

Acknowledgments*

Contents

SECTION 1

Jewelry 14

SECTION

Accessories 42

SECTION 3

Clothing 70

Introduction

Art to wear is just that—
art in the form of jewelry,
accessories or clothing. Whether it's creating original jewelry and accessories from metal, beads or found materials or adding unique and stylish touches to clothing, wearing your art lets you express your personality in a very memorable way.

I am so excited that wearable art is making a big splash once again—styles and trends of the past always seem to make a return. And they always return with a wonderful new twist. Do you remember the earrings of the eighties? Back then we couldn't get them big enough. Now we can't seem to get them long and dangly enough. In this book you'll find easy step-by-step instructions for creating fashionable necklaces, earrings, bracelets and even pins with dangle and flash that complement your personal style.

But I'm not stopping with traditional jewelry. Other trends are coming back into style for decorating clothing and accessories as well, and some of the projects in this book draw inspiration from those times. Remember all of the lace and ribbon on t-shirts and jackets from the eighties? Today's updated embellishment styles are bringing back that concept in a fresh new way. Jackets, sweaters, t-shirts and even flip-flops, jeans, purses, belts and gloves have much more personality once they've been "dressed up" a little and transformed into wearable works of art with paint, beads and even Chinese coins.

I can't think of a better way to show off your creative talents than to adorn yourself, your family and friends with your own works of art. I think you'll be thrilled with the vast array of materials, mediums and techniques used to create the projects you're about to see. You'll learn how to work with metal, wire, beads, fabric, clay and much more. In this book there is something for the young and for the young at heart. Plus the variations of each of the projects are sure to inspire you and keep you busy creating. Adorn yourself, and have fun in the process.

Basic Supplies

Each exciting project in this book will give you the chance to learn something new about working with different materials, including metal, paper, fabric and polymer clay. To make the jewelry, accessories and embellished clothing in each section, you need some specific tools and materials. Take a few minutes to read over this section to familiarize yourself with the basic supplies you'll need to have on hand. You can find most of these items at your local craft retailers. Check out your local bead and fabric stores for additional tools and materials.

Materials & Tools for Jewelry Making

Making jewelry is a wonderful outlet for your creativity because there are so many amazing beads and clasps available. Using a few basic materials and tools, you'll be able to make all of the jewelry pieces in this book.

CLASPS and **TOGGLES** are the closures used to fasten necklaces and bracelets.

END CRIMPS or **CRIMP COLLARS** are small metal pieces that can be squeezed over the end of a leather cord to allow a fastener to be attached.

EAR WIRES are used for making earrings for pierced ears. The decorative part is attached to the loop on the wire.

HEADPINS have a flat end to hold beads for drops on earrings or for dangles on necklaces.

JUMP RINGS are small circles of wire that come in a variety of sizes. They can be opened and closed to link different elements in one piece of jewelry together. For example, you can use jump rings to attach beaded drops to a chain or to each other.

CHAINS come in a variety of link sizes and shapes, from delicate to chunky.

MEMORY WIRE is a coiled wire that retains its circular shape. It comes in sizes for necklaces, bracelets and rings.

BEADS of all kinds are the cornerstone of most jewelry projects. They add color, texture and movement. Seed beads, E-beads, bicone, star, teardrop and spacer beads are examples of the beads used for this book's projects.

MINI GAME PIECES are a fun component to use for jewelry making. They are usually found with altered art supplies or with scrapbooking materials.

HANKS are several strands of beads tied together.

ROUND-NOSE PLIERS are used for shaping wire and armature wire. They are also used to create loops on the ends of wire and headpins.

NEEDLE-NOSE or **FLAT-NOSE PLIERS** are used for gripping, opening and closing jump rings and for squeezing end crimps closed.

WIRE CUTTERS are used for cutting all kinds of wire.

Materials & Tools for Working with Clay

Polymer clay is a versatile clay medium, available in a rainbow of colors. It can be used to create a variety of accessories. All clays must be baked in an oven to be properly cured. Always follow the manufacturer's instructions.

POLYMER CLAY is available in a number of brands. One brand, Fimo Soft, is a clay that is easy to work with and easy to condition. However, it is not quite as strong after baking as some other types of clay.

WIRE CUTTERS

ROUND-NOSE PLIERS

NEEDLE-NOSE PLIERS

CONDITIONING the clay means working it with your hands until it is pliable enough to shape.

PUSH MOLDS are used to press softened clay into a specific design shape.

Materials & Tools for Working with Metal

Incorporating metal into your projects adds a new dimension to the wearable art you create. For the projects in this book, you'll be working with two basic types of metal—sheets and wire.

EMBOSSING METAL SHEETS are thin metal sheets that come in a variety of weights and finishes, including copper, aluminum, brass and pewter.

WIRE is available in many colors and thicknesses. It is measured by gauge—as diameter increases, the gauge number gets smaller (and vice versa). Different projects require different types of wires and different gauges.

ARMATURE RODS (or armature wire) are thick rods that come in a variety of metals. Their thickness is measured in fractions of an inch or in millimeters. Softer aluminum armature rods are great for jewelry projects.

METAL EYELETS are small open cylinders of metal used for embellishment or to outline or reinforce punched holes. They are versatile and available in many finishes. They are great for providing strong holes for tying things.

EYELET SETTERS are used along with a hammer to secure eyelets into place.

A **RUBBER MALLET** is my favorite metal-crafting tool. By adding beads of hot glue to one end, you can create a wonderful texturing tool.

CRAFT FOAM SHEETS provide cushioning when placed under metal sheets while texturing them.

A **BRAYER** is helpful for smoothing and flattening textured metal.

A **HAMMER** is used for flattening wire and armature rods. It is also used for setting eyelets.

Materials & Tools for Working with Paper

Paper is a versatile crafting material that's great for creating collages and backgrounds. It requires only a few basic tools to make working with it easy.

SCISSORS make cutting out small shapes a breeze. Keep a good, sharp pair on hand at all times.

HOLE PUNCHES are useful for making holes in paper, metal and fabric. The most often used sizes of hole punches are 1/16" (2mm) and 1/8" (3mm). Both handheld punches and those with setting heads are available.

DECORATIVE PUNCHES cut holes in interesting shapes (like daisies or hearts) and create fun collage elements.

DÉCOUPAGE MEDIUM is a spreadable glue that dries clear in either a matte or a shiny finish. It's my favorite adhesive for paper crafts, especially for collages.

CARDSTOCK is a heavier-weight paper available in many colors, patterns, textures and finishes, ranging from smooth to heavily textured and from matte to glossy.

TEXT PAPER is a medium-weight paper available in many colors, patterns, textures and finishes.

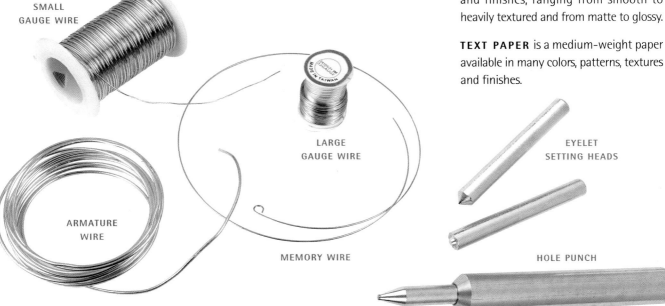

SMALL GAUGE WIRE

ARMATURE WIRE

LARGE GAUGE WIRE

MEMORY WIRE

EYELET SETTING HEADS

HOLE PUNCH

Materials & Tools for
Working with Fabric

Just like paper, fabric and fibers make interesting collages. Fabrics in colors and prints that coordinate make the perfect background for collages. Add a vintage image printed on cotton fabric to create a wonderful focal point on any object made of fabric—from a collared shirt to a tote bag.

WATER-SOLUBLE STABILIZER SHEETS are paper-thin pieces of clear material that are used to sandwich decorative fibers to create exciting embellishments.

MONOGRAMS are used to personalize your favorite garment. They are simply ironed on.

FUSIBLE WEBBING SHEETS are glue- or plastic-based transparent sheets used to bond fabric collages to background fabric. They come either encased in paper like double-sided tape or have paper on one side. They are sold by the yard, in one-yard packages or in rolls.

FABRIC GLUE is a washable glue used to adhere fabric swatches, fibers, cording, beads, buttons and any other embellishments to fabric.

STENCILS are used along with acrylic paint to apply a specific motif.

STENCIL BRUSHES are stiff-bristled brushes used to apply paint into the openings of a stencil design.

STUDS are decorative metal pieces that are attached to garments by punching a hole in the fabric. They come in many sizes and finishes.

A **STUD SETTER** is used to set studs into fabric.

An **IRON** set at medium-high heat is used to attach monograms and fusible webbing to fabric.

Miscellaneous
Supplies

Here are a few more essential supplies that you'll need for the projects in this book.

A **SELF-HEALING CUTTING MAT** with an easy-to-read grid stabilizes any material as you cut. A mat also protects your work surface and makes it easy to cut straight lines and measure width and length.

A **ROTARY CUTTER** lets you make straight, perfect cuts. It slices through fabric, paper and metal quickly and easily.

An **EMBOSSING STYLUS** is a pen-like tool with a semi-sharp tip used to trace templates, emboss and score fold lines.

ALCOHOL-BASED INKS, like Piñata colors, are used to color wood and soft metal sheets.

PERMANENT INK is used for rubber-stamping

ALCOHOL-BASED INKS

and to add color to metals and paper projects. Use a heat tool to set inks.

SCRAPBOOKING SUPPLIES include a huge selection of papers, stickers and embellishments. Look at scrapbooking materials as potential wearable art elements.

BEADING NEEDLES and **THREAD** are used to sew beaded embellishments onto garments. Make sure that the needle you buy fits through the holes in the beads you use.

A **CRAFT KNIFE** is a cutting tool with a sharp blade that is good for making small cuts in fabric and paper.

INDUSTRIAL-STRENGTH ADHESIVE, such as E-6000 craft glue, is a flexible, waterproof adhesive that dries clear. It's great for working with metal because it doesn't drip, run or rust metal.

DOUBLE-SIDED TAPE is sticky on both sides. It's clean and easy to use. Full sheets can be cut to fit any project.

A **HOT GLUE GUN** and **HOT GLUE** heats up the glue sticks to make a strong adhesive bond. You need a hot glue gun and glue sticks to create the textured rubber mallet used in the Metal Patchwork Belt project (page 62).

FABRIC FOR COLLAGES

Basic Techniques

As you create the jewelry, accessories and embellished clothing projects in this book, you'll need to know a few basic techniques. Although you'll be working on a wide variety of projects using many different materials, many of them share the same basic elements of construction. Once you're comfortable with the following techniques, you'll find the projects simple to make.

Techniques for Jewelry Making

If this is your first time making jewelry, you'll be delighted at how easy it is. Once you've learned how to make loops with round-nose jewelry pliers and how to open and close jump rings, you'll realize just how simple it is to create your own necklaces and earrings.

OPENING & CLOSING A JUMP RING

To open and close a jump ring, use needle-nose pliers to swing the ends open far enough to insert the other element. Then use the pliers to swing the ends of the jump ring closed again to safely secure the other element.

MAKING LOOPS IN HEADPINS OR WIRES

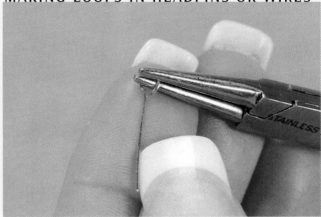

Allow approximately ⅜" (1cm) of wire above the beads for the loop (more for larger loops). Use round-nose pliers to bend the wire to a 45° angle. Grip the end of the wire and roll it around the nose of the pliers to form a loop.

MAKING A WRAPPED LOOP

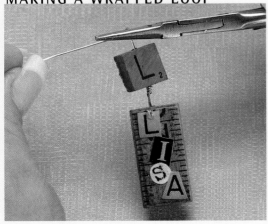

1 *Using round-nose pliers, grip the wire ⅛" (3mm) above the bead and bend the wire to form a right angle.*

2 *Bend the wire tail around the pliers to form a loop. Grip the loop with the pliers, and wrap the wire tail around the base wire three times. Trim the excess from the tail with wire cutters.*

Techniques for Metal & Wire Work

Working with metal and wire makes creating sophisticated-looking jewelry and embellishments easy. All you have to do is learn a few simple techniques and you'll be able to texture metal and twist and hammer wire into any shape you desire.

MAKING SPIRALS & SHAPES

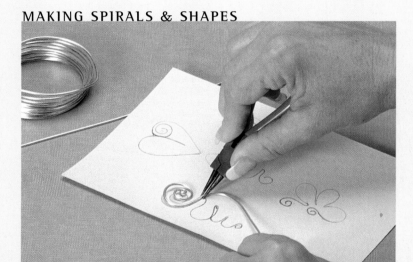

Grip the end of the wire or armature rod with round-nose pliers and twist to form a small loop. Hold the loop with the pliers and continue to twist the remaining length of wire around it with your free hand, forming a spiral. To follow a pattern, simply place the wire over the pattern and bend the wire along the lines indicated. You may need to grip the wire in certain places in order to create tight turns.

TEXTURING METAL

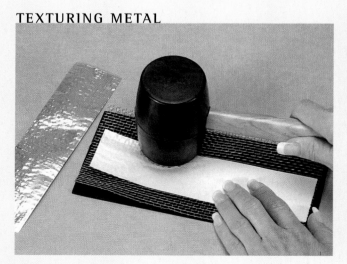

Place a metal 8 mesh screen onto a sheet of craft foam. Place the metal on the screen face down and hammer it with the textured mallet. Experiment with different mesh counts to find the one you like best.

FLATTENING METAL

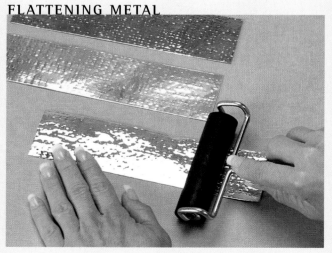

After texturing metal, either with the textured mallet or by crumpling it in your hand, the material must be smoothed out before it can be used for any project. Simply lay the piece of textured metal on a flat, smooth surface and roll over it with the brayer. The metal will be flat but still textured when you are done.

HAMMERING WIRE & ARMATURE RODS

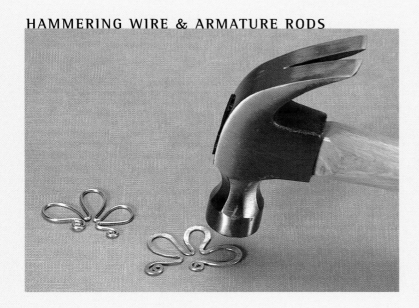

After you create a design with wire or an armature rod, place it on a durable surface and flatten it by tapping the entire piece repeatedly with a hammer.

PUNCHING HOLES & SETTING EYELETS

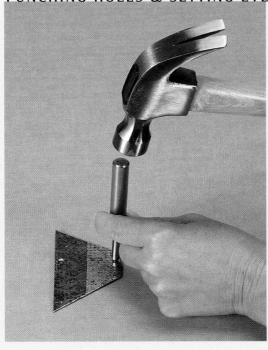
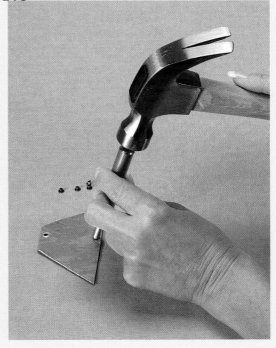

1 *Using a hole punch and eyelet setter with interchangeable heads allows you to punch holes and set eyelets anywhere on a project through any kind of material. Before punching the hole, make sure to mark its placement. Set the material to be punched on a cutting mat. Using the hole punch head and a hammer, punch the holes by lightly tapping the head with the hammer.*

2 *Insert the eyelets from the front so that the "lip" or rim of the eyelet outlines the hole. Turn the project over and use the setting head and a hammer to set the eyelets from the back by gently hitting the setting head with the hammer until the eyelet shaft spreads.*

When you think of "art to wear," the first thing that probably comes to mind is jewelry. You might be intimidated by the idea of making your own jewelry, but it's really quite easy. Once you know a few simple jewelry-making techniques and have some easy-to-find materials (see page 8), you can create almost anything. Each project in this section teaches you a new technique that you can use in future jewelry-making adventures. (Make sure to check out the variations at the end of each project for inspiration.)

For many of the projects in this section, you'll make jewelry out of multi-media materials, such as dimensional words traditionally used for scrapbooking in the Say-It-With-Jewelry Anklet and even miniature game pieces, as in the Game Pieces Jewelry. Other pieces use beads and colored metal for flash and flare. There's a Memory Wire Necklace with showy dangles that plays on a more "traditional" notion of wearable art, and you'll love making a few of the colorful and catchy Metallic Bangles to stack on your arm.

Jewelry

For this poetic piece, you can choose words that encourage, amuse or simply express what you feel. These great dimensional word stickers are made to embellish scrapbook pages, but when I saw them, jewelry was on my mind. What a great way to say what you feel and wear it proudly. Or spell out a special message for a friend or family member, and she'll always think of you when she wears her personalized anklet.

Say-It-With-Jewelry Anklet

MATERIALS AND TOOLS

pewter embossing metal sheet,
3" x 4" (8cm x 10cm)

self-adhesive dimensional word stickers,
commonly used for scrapbooking

about 10" (25cm) linked jewelry chain

charms and/or beads

silver headpins

silver jump rings

silver spring clasp

emery board

$1/16$" (2mm) hole punch

wire cutters

round-nose jewelry pliers

scissors

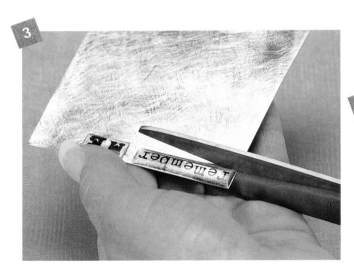

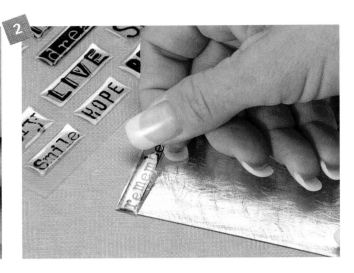

1 Cut and sand metal sheet

With scissors, cut a 3" x 4" (8cm x 10cm) rectangle of pewter embossing metal. Using an emery board, sand the metal surface in a circular motion.

2 Adhere word stickers to metal sheet

Select which words you want to use for the anklet from the sheet of self-adhesive dimensional word stickers. Peel the word stickers that you choose from the carrier sheet and adhere them to the rectangle of pewter embossing metal so that the top edge of each sticker aligns with the top edge of the metal piece. Leave enough space to cut between the two stickers.

3 Cut out words

Cut the adhered words out of the metal sheet with scissors, trimming right along the perimeter of the stickers.

4 Punch holes on sides of words

Use a 1/16" (2mm) hole punch to punch holes on the left and right sides of the first word sticker you chose.

5 Connect words

Use a 1/16" (2mm) hole punch to punch a hole at the bottom center of the first word sticker and a hole at the top center of the second word sticker. Align the holes, then connect the two words with a jump ring.

6 Cut chain and add words

With wire cutters, cut two 4" (10cm) lengths of linked chain. (You may need to adjust the length of the chains you use depending on the length of the word sticker and the diameter of your ankle.) Use jump rings to attach one piece of chain to both the left and right sides of the first word accent, leaving the second word dangling.

8 Add charms

Add charms, beads or other accent pieces onto the chain links, if desired. To make a dangle, slide the beads you select onto a headpin. Trim the wire, leaving about $^3/_8$" (1cm) above the beads. Using the round-nose jewelry pliers, make a loop around one of the links in the chain with the headpin wire and wrap the excess wire around the headpin (see Basic Techniques, page 11). Repeat for all bead/charm dangles.

7 Add spring clasps

Add jump rings to either end of the linked chain. Then attach a spring clasp to the right jump ring.

*Finished Anklet

What a perfect gift! Make it for yourself, or give it to someone special. With so many different dimensional words available, the poetic possibilities are endless.

*MORE FUN
Art to Wear

Using the same jewelry-making techniques, you can create a necklace and a pair of earrings to complete the set. Experiment with color, length and number of dangles for a completely different project every time.

This necklace is made from memory wire, a wire that keeps its coiled shape even when it is unraveled and cut. Memory wire comes in different-sized coils and is measured by the number of coils (instead of by inches or centimeters). You choose the beads that give this necklace a unique look—elegant and sophisticated or fun and casual. Whatever style you choose, you're bound to be remembered when you wear this dramatic piece.

Memory Wire Necklace

MATERIALS AND TOOLS

1½ coils of necklace-sized memory wire

silver headpins

1 set of ear wires

36" (91cm) of 24-gauge wire

crystal E-beads

crystal bicone beads

crystal teardrop beads

crystal star beads

wire cutters

round-nose jewelry pliers

FOLLOW THIS DIAGRAM AS YOU CREATE THE DANGLES FOR THIS SOPHISTICATED
NECKLACE. REFER TO STEP NINE ON PAGE 24 AS YOU ASSEMBLE EACH DANGLE.

key

○   E-bead

◇   bicone bead

✳   star bead

△   teardrop bead

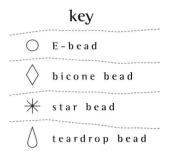

1 Cut wire and loop end

Cut a piece of memory wire, allowing it to curl around 1½ times before
snipping it with wire cutters. Use round-nose jewelry pliers to create a
small loop at one end of the wire to hold the beads you'll be stringing on
(see Basic Techniques, page 11).

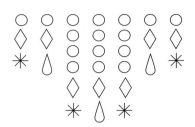

2 Bead wire

String crystal E-beads onto the other end of the wire, continuing until
the entire length of wire is beaded.

3 Loop end

Secure the beads by creating a small loop at the open end of the wire
using the round-nose jewelry pliers.

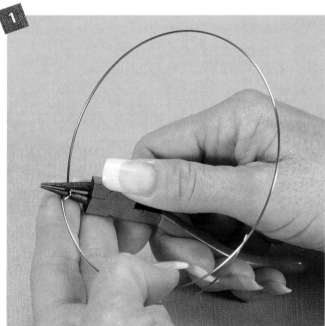

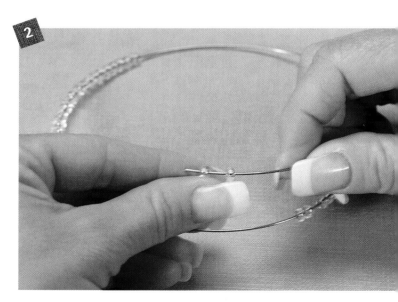

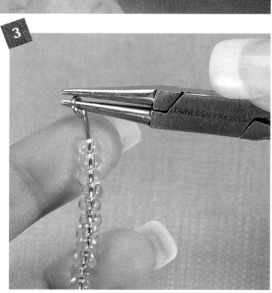

4 Cut and loop wire lengths

Cut twenty-three ⅞" (2cm) lengths of 24-gauge wire. Create a very small loop at one end of each length by using the round-nose jewelry pliers to curl the wire.

5 Wire E-beads and bicone beads

String one crystal E-bead onto a ⅞" (2mm) wire length. Loop the other end to secure the bead. Repeat for fifteen more E-beads and seven bicone beads.

6 Wire teardrop beads

Slide one crystal teardrop bead onto a silver headpin, then use the round-nose pliers to loop the sharp end and secure the bead. Repeat for two more teardrop beads.

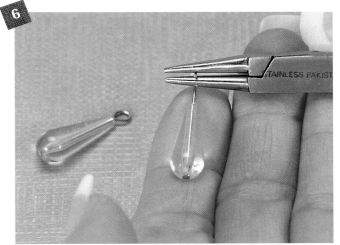

Tip* *Make a black mark on the jewelry pliers where you grasp the tip of the wire to ensure that the loops are always uniform.*

7 Wire star beads

Slide one crystal star bead onto a silver headpin. Trim the wire so that ⅜" (1cm) of wire remains. Repeat for three more star beads.

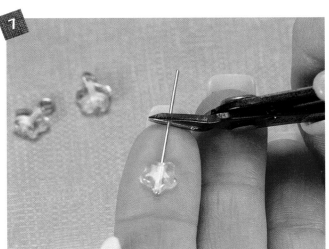

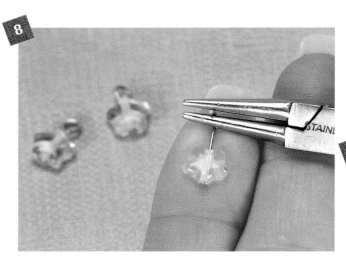

8 Secure star beads

Loop the end of each headpin wire with round-nose pliers to secure the star beads.

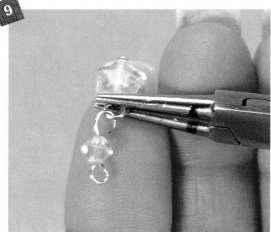

9 Create dangles

Connect the beads together to create seven dangles, following the diagram (see page 22). To connect the beads, use pliers to open a loop on one end of a beaded wire, connect it to a loop on another beaded wire, and then close the loop to secure.

10 Lay out dangles

Lay out the body of the necklace, then place the dangles in position.

11 Attach center dangle

Eyeball the center of the necklace, then open the end loop of the longest dangle with jewelry pliers and hook it onto the necklace wire. Close the opened link with the jewelry pliers to secure the dangle.

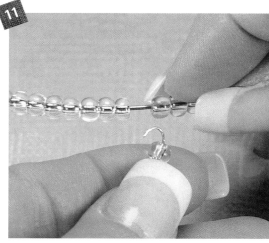

12 Add remaining dangles

Add three dangles to each side of the center dangle, spacing them each three beads apart, again referring to the diagram (see page 22).

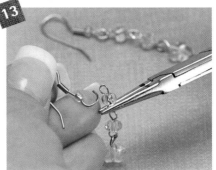

13 Make earrings

Using the same technique as used in making the dangles for the necklace, create two more dangles for earrings. With the jewelry pliers, unhook the bottom loop of an ear wire. Slide on a single E-bead. Then insert the top loop of a dangle and close the ear wire loop to secure. Repeat for the remaining earring.

*Finished Necklace & Earrings

This sophisticated necklace and earring set adds just the right amount of dangle to set off the scoop or v-neckline of your favorite dress or blouse. Be sure to experiment with different colors and styles of beads in your next project.

*MORE FUN Art to Wear

Using the same techniques to create a completely different look, make a beaded memory wire necklace to slide around the brim of a hat.

The game is on, so spell it out. For these playful pieces, you'll spell out your own name (or some-one else's) to personalize a necklace, bracelet or earrings. This project (and its variations) combines the fun of miniature game pieces with the vintage style of aged papers and alphabets by turning scrap-booking materials into jewelry.

Game Pieces Jewelry

MATERIALS AND TOOLS

small wooden game pieces
(domino, die, letter tile)
AVAILABLE IN CRAFT STORES WITH
ALTERED ART AND SCRAPBOOKING SUPPLIES

yellow alcohol-based ink,
like Piñata ink in Sunbright Yellow

ruler motif decorative scrapbooking paper

assorted letter stickers
STICKER SHEETS, FOUND IN CRAFT STORES
WITH SCRAPBOOKING SUPPLIES

2 6mm amber beads

2 gold spacer beads

20" (51cm) of 24-gauge silver wire

18" (46cm) of 1mm black leather cord

2 crimp collars

heart toggle clasp

jump rings

découpage medium

hand drill with $^1/_{16}$" (2mm) drill bit

paintbrush or disposable glue brush

needle-nose pliers

round-nose jewelry pliers

wire cutters

scissors

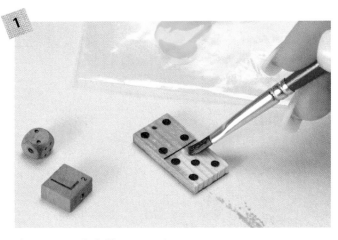

1 Stain and drill game pieces

Select your wooden game pieces—a domino, a die and a letter tile. Stain the game pieces by brushing the yellow alcohol-based ink over the entire surface of each piece. Allow the pieces to dry. Drill a hole into the top of each piece, drilling through the top edge of the die and the letter tile and through the front (upper center) of the domino.

2 Adhere ruler paper to domino

Cut a strip of the ruler motif scrapbooking paper to fit onto the surface of the domino piece. Coat the back of the paper strip with the découpage medium and adhere it to the back of the domino.

3 Collage letters

Spell out a word or name using self-adhesive scrapbooking letter stickers. If desired, cut the letters out to vary the shape of each sticker. Run the letters vertically down the papered side of the domino piece, overlapping as desired. Brush the domino with the découpage medium to seal the collage.

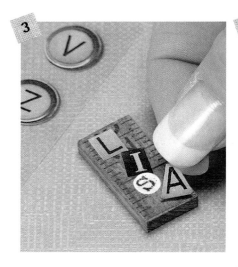

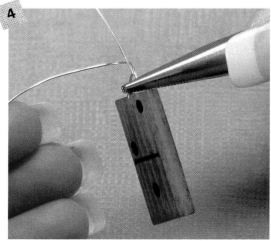

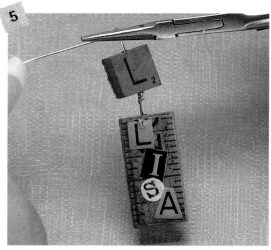

4 Wire domino

Cut a 10" (25cm) length of 24-gauge wire. Run the wire through the hole in the domino piece and allow about 2" (5cm) of the wire to come through on one side. Where the 2" (5cm) length comes through the hole, use your fingers to bend the wire up and criss-cross it with the length of wire on the other side. Using needle-nose pliers, grip just below where the wires cross. Hold the game pieces and wire steady, then wrap the short end of the wire around the long end three times (see Basic Techniques, page 11). Trim the short wire after wrapping.

5 Secure letter tile

Slide the letter tile onto the same piece of wire, directly on top of the wrapped wire above the domino piece. With round-nose jewelry pliers, grip the wire ⅛" (3mm) above the hole in the tile. Loop the wire around the tip of the pliers, then wrap the remaining length around the base of the loop three times. Trim off excess wire.

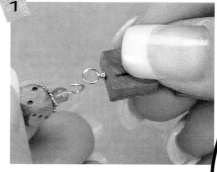

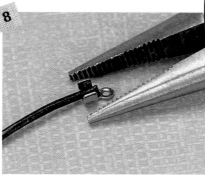

6 Wire die and beads

Cut a 3" (8cm) length of 24-gauge wire. Grip the end of the wire with the round-nose jewelry pliers, then bend the wire up and around to form a small loop. Slide one amber bead, one gold spacer bead, the die, another gold bead and another amber bead onto the wire. Then loop the end of the wire to secure the beads. Trim the wire if necessary.

7 Connect all game pieces

Open a loop on one end of the beaded die piece (from step 6) and connect it to the loop at the top of the letter tile. Close the loop to secure.

8 Add crimp ends and toggles

Cut an 18" (45cm) length of leather cord. Attach a crimp collar to one end of the cord using the needle-nose pliers. Connect a jump ring to the crimp, then attach the heart toggle clasp to the jump ring. Slide the game piece pendant onto the cord, then add a crimp, jump ring and the other half of the toggle to the other end of the cord.

*Finished Necklace

That's your name, so wear it out. Continue the shabby chic theme by pairing this altered art-style necklace with an old pair of jeans and a t-shirt.

*MORE FUN Art to Wear

Make necklaces for all of your friends, adding their names to personalize the jewelry. Create a game pieces bracelet to complete the set.

Vinyl tubing is used as the base material beneath the glittery surface of these fashionable bangles. Covering the tubing with ink-dyed soft metal sheets creates an exciting shimmery effect that makes this simple-to-make project look impressive. You'll love experimenting with different patterns of color to give each bangle a unique dimension.

Metallic Bangles

MATERIALS AND TOOLS

extra-fine embossing metal sheet,
6" x 6" (15cm x 15cm), gold on
one side and silver on the other

blue, magenta and yellow alcohol-based inks,
like Piñata ink in Baja Blue,
Señorita Magenta and Sunbright Yellow

plastic tubing ¼" (6mm) in diameter
AVAILABLE AT HARDWARE STORES
AND AQUARIUM STORES

sheet of peel-and-stick double-sided tape

cotton swab

rubbing alcohol

spray bottle

sea sponge

embossing heat gun

brayer

cutting mat

rotary cutter

ruler

scissors

1 Spray alcohol onto metal sheet

Pour some rubbing alcohol into the spray bottle. Lay the metal embossing sheet flat on your work surface, gold side up, then spray the sheet with rubbing alcohol.

2 Add ink

Squeeze a few drops of each ink color onto the metal sheet, randomly spacing the drops and allowing the ink to spread.

3 Sponge alcohol onto inked surface

Spray a sea sponge with alcohol until damp. Blot the sea sponge up and down on the metal sheet, working the alcohol across the inked surface in horizontal rows. Be careful not to overwork the colors.

4 Heat set surface

Heat the inked surface of the metal sheet for about two minutes with an embossing heat gun, keeping the gun moving over the surface until the ink is dry.

5 Respray and reset surface

Spray the sheet with alcohol again, then set the surface with an embossing heat gun. If you are not satisfied with the result, spray and heat the sheet one more time. Allow the sheet to cool.

6 Crumple sheet

Lightly crumple the sheet to give it a crinkled texture.

7 Flatten textured sheet

Uncrumple the sheet and lay it out on your work surface. Roll a brayer over the sheet to flatten it. The sheet should now be flat but textured.

8 Cut sheet

On a cutting mat, use a rotary cutter to cut 1" (3cm) wide strips from the metal sheet.

9 Adhere tape to metal

Cut 1" x 8½" (3cm x 22cm) strips from a sheet of peel-and-stick double-sided tape. Peel the carrier sheet off of one side of the tape strip and lay it sticky side up on your work surface. Then adhere a metal strip to the exposed sticky side, aligning the edges. Add a partial metal strip to cover the remainder of the tape strip, overlapping the first piece of metal slightly.

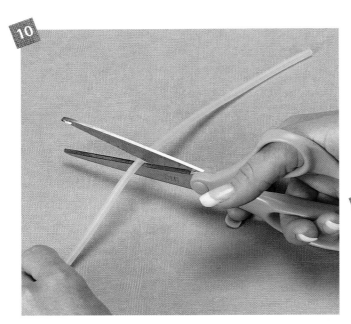

10 Cut plastic tubing

Use scissors to cut an 8½" (22cm) length of plastic tubing.

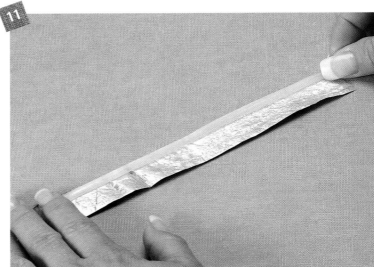

11 Adhere metal strip to tubing

Peel the paper backing from the back of the metal strip that is already attached to the double-sided tape (from step 9). Be careful when you peel away the paper; because the metal sheet is so thin, it tends to curl up and stick to itself. Lay the metal strip adhesive side up on your work surface. Place the plastic tubing right along the long edge of the metal strip.

12 Cover tubing

With your fingers, roll the tubing until it is completely wrapped in the metal strip. Keep rolling until the metal strip is completely adhered to the tubing.

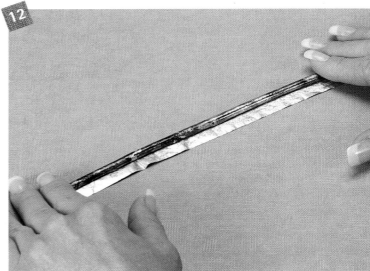

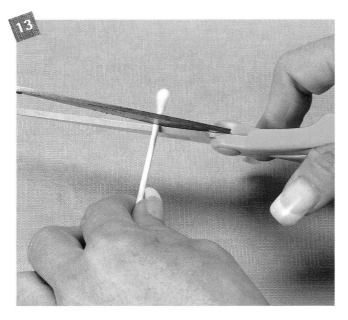

13 Cut cotton swab

Cut the cotton tip off of a cotton swab. Cut the remaining stick into a 1" (3cm) piece.

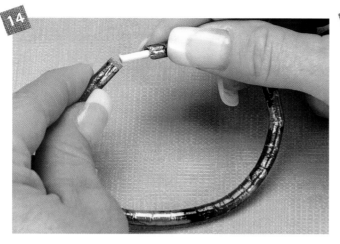

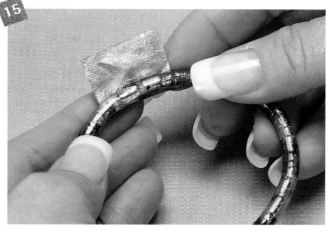

14 Form ring

Insert half of the 1" (3cm) cotton swab piece into one end of the tubing. Bring the tubing around and slide it onto the other half of the swab piece until the two ends of tubing meet. The tube will fit securely over the swab, securing the bangle.

15 Adhere metal strip to tubing

Cut a 1" (3cm) square piece from an adhesive-backed metal strip. Wrap the piece of sticky metal around the tubing, concealing and securing the seam.

*Finished Bangles

These bangles are so quick and easy you'll want to make a few of them. Mix them with a few gold bangles for a sophisticated stack.

*MORE FUN
Art to Wear

You can cover almost any surface with metal sheets—earrings, necklaces, even shoes! To make these metallic mules, simply cut a strip of inked metal to the size of the toe strap and glue it on. Embellish with gold studs and gold frames.

I love altered art, and this pin is a miniature version. To create a perfect background for this whimsical piece, you'll use pages from an old book. Add just a few items of ephemera to complete the collage and let your pin tell a story. I like to find old books and ephemera elements at used book stores and yard sales—every element brings with it a history that comes to life in the finished piece.

Paper Collage Pin

MATERIALS AND TOOLS

old book to cut up

collage sources, including magazines, stamps and vintage photographs

pigment ink, rust

10" (25cm) of 20-gauge copper wire

20" (51cm) of 24-gauge copper wire

decorative amber beads in a variety of shapes and sizes

pin back

brass-colored eyelets

découpage medium

thin-tipped permanent marker

paintbrush

brayer

decorative punches, such as a daisy punch

eyelet setter with hole punch

hammer

cutting mat

round-nose jewelry pliers

industrial-strength adhesive or glue made for metal, such as E-6000

rotary cutter

scissors or craft knife

ruler

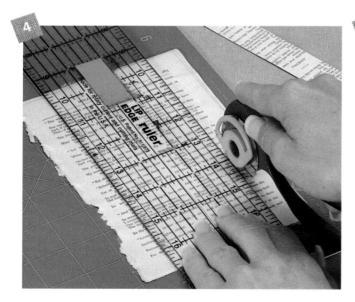

1 Coat page with découpage medium

Remove about five pages from an old book. Using a paintbrush, coat one side of one page with découpage medium.

2 Create stack of pages

Place another page on top of the glue-coated surface, then run a brayer across the top page to eliminate any air bubbles. Coat the surface with découpage medium, add another page and smooth it with the brayer. Continue until all the pages are adhered together in a stack.

3 Découpage both sides of stack

Coat the front page with découpage medium and let it dry. Repeat for the back page. Let the entire stack dry.

4 Cut stack into strips

On a cutting mat, use a rotary cutter to cut the dried stacked pages vertically into 1" (3cm) wide strips. Cut the strips into 3" (8cm) lengths.

5 Apply pigment ink

Dab a paintbrush into the rust ink pad, then brush the ink onto both sides of the 1" x 3" (3cm x 8cm) strips, allowing the first side to dry before inking the other side. The ink will reveal the texture of the glue brushstrokes on the surface.

6 Cut out collage elements

Select elements for your collage using sources such as magazines, stamps and vintage photographs. Use scissors or a craft knife to cut out the elements. If desired, add some interest by tearing the edges of a few elements. You can also use a decorative punch, such as a daisy punch, to cut text or images into interesting shapes.

7 Apply collage elements

Lay a strip of stacked and inked paper vertically on your work surface. Arrange the elements you cut out on the strip, moving them around to create a pleasing composition. Lift, tuck and overlap the elements for a collaged look. Brush découpage medium onto the back of each element and begin adhering them to the strip. Use a small paintbrush to add the smallest pieces.

8 Finish and seal collage

Add the final elements to your collage. When your collage is complete, coat the front and the back of the strip with découpage medium to seal the ink and other elements.

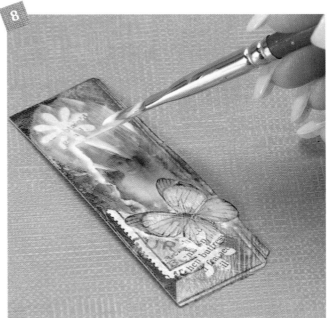

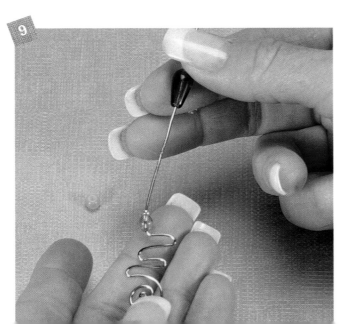

9 Scroll and bead accent piece

Cut a 7½" (19cm) length of 20-gauge copper wire. Use round-nose jewelry pliers to scroll one end of the wire in a decorative design (see Basic Techniques, page 12). After scrolling half of the wire, thread a few decorative amber beads onto the unscrolled end.

10 Finish scrolling accent piece

Scroll the remaining half of the wire, securing the beads in the middle. Create two more smaller accent pieces in the same manner.

11 Flatten scrolled wire

Use a hammer to pound and flatten the scrolled wire on all three accent pieces.

12 Punch holes for eyelets

Lay out the accent pieces with the collaged piece, positioning them next to the edges where you'd like them attached. Mark the spots for the holes with a thin-tipped permanent marker directly onto the collaged strip. Position the hole punch head over each mark and pound the top of it with a hammer to make the hole (see Basic Techniques, page 13). You should have two holes for the top piece, two holes for the side piece and one hole for the bottom piece.

13 Set eyelets

Insert the eyelets through the front of the collaged piece so that the flat rim is face up. Turn the piece over and use the setting head and a hammer to set eyelets in all of the holes.

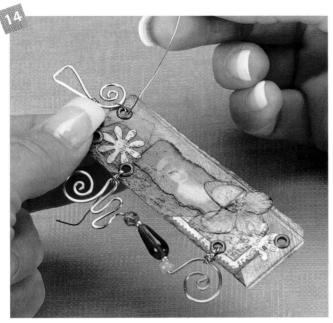

14 Attach accent pieces

Cut a workable length of 24-gauge copper wire, long enough for wiring the accents onto the collage, or about 18" (46cm) for each accent piece. Wrap the wire through each hole and around each scroll two to three times. Wrap the tail of the wire around the looped wire between the accent piece and the pin itself a few times to secure. Repeat until all of the accent pieces are secured.

15 Attach pin back

Glue a pin back onto the back of the collage piece. Rather than using wet craft glue, which can sometimes rust metal, use a glue made for metals, such as E-6000, for attaching jewelry findings to surfaces.

*MORE FUN
Art to Wear

If a pin isn't quite your style, you can create a pendant instead. You can experiment with different colors of pigment ink to make each collage unique. Follow the same steps as for creating a pin, making sure to attach a scrolled metal accent piece at the top of the pendant to thread the chain or leather cord through to make it a necklace.

*Finished
Pin

Just imagine the vintage flare this pin will add to a stylish denim jacket. Or you can wear it on the lapel of a blazer to add a whimsical accent to a business suit.

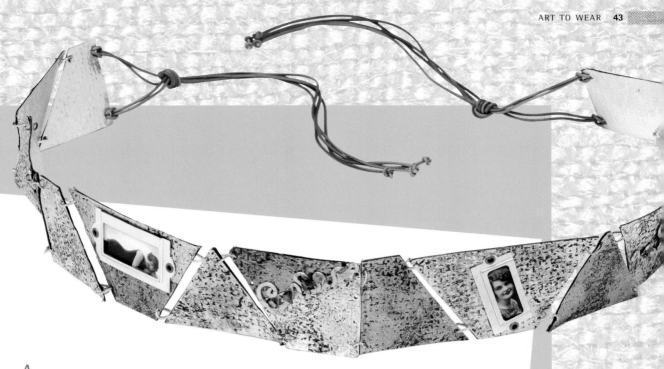

Accessories make it possible to dress up an outfit by adding some unexpected color, a little glitz, a punch of fun and a lot of style. In fact, accessories are often the most important part of an ensemble. The projects in this section will spice up your wardrobe and allow you to express your funky and cool personality by showing you how to add unique touches to your outfits.

Do you have a tried-and-true outfit that you love, but one that could use a dash of panache? Add a little Pocket Jewelry to jeans or pair the Metal Patchwork Belt with a monochromatic top and slacks, and you'll automatically transform your clothing. Or make the Scrolled Flip-Flops, Painted Leather Gloves or Clay Face Purse to pull together the look of any outfit. Have fun with these simple and elegant projects, and don't be afraid to add your own creative spin.

Accessories

Pocket Jewelry can go anywhere—it can be dressy or casual depending on the beads and charms you choose. It's a trendy accessory that will let you add your own personal flare to your favorite pair of jeans—whether they're baggy and riddled with holes or brand-new hip-huggers.

Pocket Jewelry

MATERIALS AND TOOLS

pair of jeans or shorts

10" (25cm) linked chain
AVAILABLE IN HARDWARE STORES

assorted black, silver and
colored beads and charms

10–12 silver headpins

2 lobster claw clasps

silver jump rings, $^1/_8$" and $^1/_4$"
(3mm and 6mm)

$^1/_{16}$" (2mm) hole punch

round-nose jewelry pliers

needle-nose pliers

wire cutters

1 Bead headpins

Thread beads and charms onto ten to twelve silver headpins, placing two or three assorted beads and/or charms on each headpin. Push the beads down to the head and trim each headpin about ⅜" (1cm) above the last bead with the wire cutters.

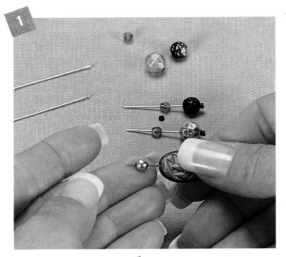

2 Loop headpins, create dangles

With round-nose jewelry pliers, grip the sharp end of the headpin. Twist the end over to form a small loop. Repeat for all beaded headpins.

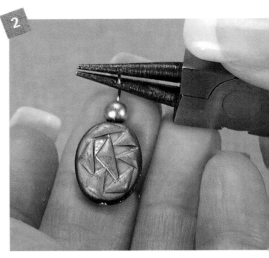

Tip* *Using the materials listed, you will make Pocket Jewelry for one pocket. Please double the amounts of linked chain, beads, headpins, clasps and jump rings to make Pocket Jewelry for two pockets.*

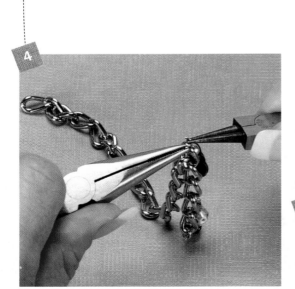

3 Cut chain and position beads

Cut a 7½" (19cm) length of linked chain. (You can use small wire cutters to cut the chain or use pliers to open and pull off links at the appropriate spot.) Lay out the chain on your work surface, and then place the dangles under the chain in the order you want them to be attached.

4 Attach dangles to chain

Use round-nose jewelry pliers to attach a jump ring to each dangle loop. Following the arrangement that you laid out in step 3, use round-nose jewelry pliers to attach the dangles to the appropriate links in the chain. Squeeze the ⅛" (3mm) jump rings closed with the round-nose jewelry pliers after connecting each dangle.

5 Attach jump rings and clasps

Attach a lobster claw clasp to each end of the chain using a ⅛" (3mm) jump ring.

6 Attach jump rings to denim

Use a ¹/₁₆" (2mm) hole punch to punch two sets of two holes through the fabric, just below either end of each front pocket. Attach a ¼" (6mm) jump ring through each set of holes.

7 Attach chain to jump rings

Attach the chain to the jump rings on the pocket with the lobster claw clasps. Repeat for the second pocket.

*MORE FUN Art to Wear

You can also dress up a plain hoodie sweatshirt by making a zipper pull with the same beads and charms attached to a linked chain used in the Pocket Jewelry project.

*Finished Pocket Jewelry

These jeans have gone from bleak to chic with these carefully placed beaded chains. And thanks to the lobster claw attachment, you can even make a few different chains using different color schemes to coordinate your jeans with multiple tops. Simply detach one chain and replace it with another. Remove the chains before washing the jeans.

Add flare to your next pair of flip-flops with these simply striking scrolled metal designs. Using an easy hammered-wire technique and a few beads, you'll create a playful asymmetrical design that will take standard summer thongs from humdrum to fantastic. Check out the variation projects as well—the embellishment possibilities for scrolled metal accents are limitless.

Scrolled Flip-Flops

MATERIALS AND TOOLS

scroll templates
SEE PAGE 50

1 pair of flip-flops

36" (91cm) of $^1/_{16}$" (2mm)
aluminum armature wire

a workable length
(18" to 24" [45cm-60cm])
of 32-gauge silver beading wire

assorted amber beads

gold seed beads

$^1/_{16}$" (2mm) hole punch

hammer

round-nose jewelry pliers

wire cutters

industrial-strength adhesive or
glue made for metal, such as E-6000

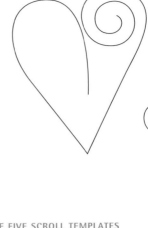

THESE PATTERNS ARE FULL SIZE. USE THESE FIVE SCROLL TEMPLATES
TO SHAPE THE ARMATURE WIRE ACCENTS THAT WILL BE ATTACHED
TO THE FLIP-FLOPS (SEE STEP 1, BELOW).

1 Cut and shape wire

Cut four 8" (20cm) lengths of armature wire (more if you want to make more than four accent pieces). Use a small pair of round-nose jewelry pliers to bend, twist and scroll the wire into the shapes on the template above, or design your own shapes, if space is an issue (see Basic Techniques, page 12).

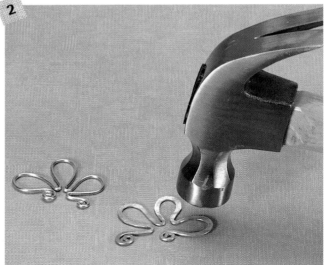

2 Flatten scrolled accent pieces

Use a large hammer to pound the scrolled armature wire piece until it is flattened (see Basic Techniques, page 13). Repeat for each accent piece.

3 Place accent piece on strap

Position an accent piece against one flip-flop strap as desired. Holding the piece in place, use a $1/16$" (2mm) hole punch to punch a few holes on the strap alongside the accent piece.

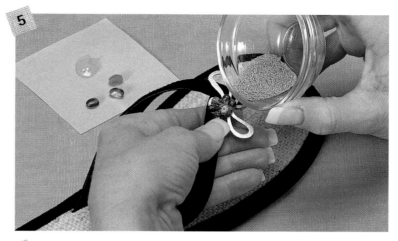

4 Attach accent pieces with wire

Knot the end of a piece of 32-gauge silver beading wire. Thread the wire through the first hole, pulling it taut with the knot in the back. To secure the first accent piece to the strap, stitch the wire around the piece by pulling the wire in and out of the holes on the strap and around the metal piece. When finished, tie another knot to secure, then trim off any excess wire. Add other accent pieces in the same manner.

5 Embellish with beads

Apply a small amount of glue to the center of the accent piece, then press assorted amber beads into the glue. Pour seed beads over the area to cover any excess glue. Repeat with each accent piece, as desired.

6 Finish other flip-flop

Repeat steps 3–5 with the other flip-flop, adding accent pieces and beads as desired.

*Finished Flip-Flops

Adding only one accent piece on the second flip-flop accentuates the playfulness of this design. Experiment with making different spiraled shapes of your own design.

*MORE FUN
Art to Wear

Now that you've seen how easy it is to add hammered-wire embellishments, don't stop with just flip-flops. You can decorate cell phone cases, earrings and necklaces using the same techniques and materials as in this project.

Make your warm winter gloves cool by adding an abstract brushstroke design that highlights the rich texture and color of the leather. This project takes bright-colored paints to create a dramatic motif of curving lines that varies slightly from glove to glove. This piece of colorful wearable art will brighten up even the bleakest of winter days.

Painted Leather Gloves

MATERIALS AND TOOLS

pair of black leather gloves

acrylic paints in bright, coordinating colors, like metallic copper, metallic red, metallic peach, citron green and bright blue

no. 8 shader flat paintbrush

palette paper

dish of water

1 Paint copper strokes

Squeeze out all of the paint colors onto palette paper. Load
the brush with copper paint, then paint a basic comma stroke
onto the glove. To create the comma stroke, hold the chisel tip
of the paintbrush at a 90° angle to the surface of the glove.
Push the tip down onto the surface to create a thick stroke,
then lift and pull the brush down and to the left as you lighten
the stroke to thin out the line. Paint three comma strokes on
the right side, spacing them ½" (1cm) apart. Add two quick,
thin strokes on the left, parallel to each other and intersecting
the comma strokes (as pictured in step 2).

2 Add peach strokes

Rinse the brush in a dish of water to remove the previous
paint color, and then blot it on a paper towel to dry it. With
peach paint, apply comma strokes to the surface of the glove,
placing two in between the copper strokes and two others
that mirror the design. Paint two thin parallel strokes that
intersect the bottom of the parallel copper strokes.

3 Add red strokes

With red paint, use the chiseled edge of the brush to add a very fine line
of color next to each copper stroke.

4 Add green strokes

Add lines of green paint next to every peach stroke, except the lower parallel line.

5 Add blue strokes

Add very fine lines of blue paint to accent the final composition.

6 Paint other glove

Paint a variation of the design on the other glove, altering the composition to make the gloves similar but slightly different.

*Finished Gloves

Say goodbye to plain black gloves—who said warm had to be drab? Remember—it's always OK to add your own creative touches, so feel free to pick different paint colors. For example, using several shades from the same color family would be an interesting twist on this project.

*MORE FUN Art to Wear

If you like this project, you can apply the same painted motif to a hard eyeglass case and make it into an evening purse by attaching some simple hardware and a chain.

Let's face it, having the perfect evening bag always makes you look put together for a night out. And this one has it all—character, texture, dimension and one-of-a-kind style. What more could you want? You'll be delighted at how easy it is to work with polymer clay, and the beading techniques used to embellish around the face add great impact. When you finish this project you'll feel like a true artist.

Clay Face Purse

MATERIALS AND TOOLS

metallic gold polymer clay
(FIMO SOFT)

moon face push mold, like Amaco's
Maureen Carlson moon series push molds

small black purse

metallic paste, like Amaco's
Patina Rub 'n Buff

metallic powdered pigment,
like Pearl Ex Super Russet

purple acrylic paint, like
Plaid FolkArt's Metallic Amethyst

black acrylic paint

hank of mixed blue and purple seed beads

assorted beads in blue, turquoise and purple

gold seed beads

Chinese coins

small decorative feather

fabric swatches in various colors and patterns

gold leafing pen

palette paper or piece of paper for paint

cornstarch or baby powder

rubbing alcohol

needle tool for gluing on beads
AVAILABLE IN THE POLYMER CLAY
SECTION OF YOUR CRAFT STORE

washable fabric glue

plastic sandwich bag

industrial-strength adhesive or
glue made for metal, such as E-6000

paintbrushes

oven

Tip* *Before you begin working with polymer clay, make sure that your hands and all work surfaces are clean—the clay will attract dirt.*

Before rolling your clay into a ball, make sure to condition it. Simply knead the clay with your hands, working it until it is soft and pliable. You can create snakes, twist the clay or flatten it into a pancake to condition it.

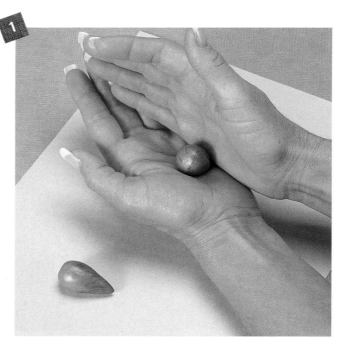

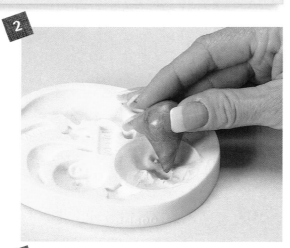

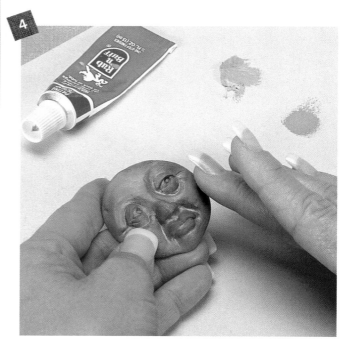

1 Form cone from polymer clay

Roll a small piece of polymer clay between the palms of your hands to form a ball about ¾" (2cm) in diameter. Then shape the clay ball into a cone by rolling one end of it between the heels of your hands (see Basic Supplies, pages 8-9).

2 Press clay into powdered mold

With a paintbrush, coat the mold with cornstarch or baby powder. Press the clay cone into the mold, point side down so that the clay will reach the bottom crevices of the nose and eyes. Continue pressing the clay until the back surface is flat and even.

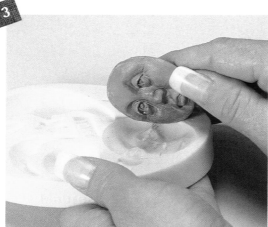

3 Remove clay from mold and bake

Remove the clay from the mold by simply bending it—the flex mold is soft and pliable, so just twisting it slightly will allow the clay to pop right out. Bake in a 265°F (129°C) oven for 30 minutes. Let the clay cool completely. (Read the manufacturer's instructions for specific baking directions.)

4 Gild one side of clay face

Squeeze a small amount of metallic paste onto a palette or piece of paper. Dab your finger in the paste, then rub the paste across one half of the face to highlight the raised areas of the molded surface. When finished, you can remove the metallic paste from your finger with rubbing alcohol.

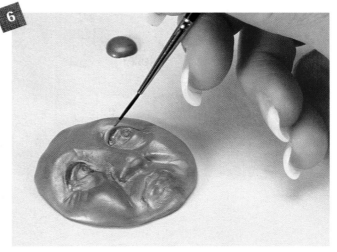

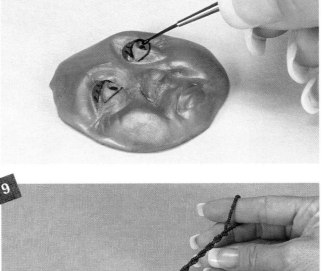

5 Gild other side of clay face

Use a small paintbrush to apply metallic powder across the other half of the face, again highlighting the raised areas.

6 Paint eyelids

Paint the eyelids with metallic purple acrylic paint.

7 Add eye details

With black acrylic paint, outline the top and bottom eyelids. Paint in the center of the eye and add eyelashes. Repeat for the other eye.

8 Knot bead hanks

Pull a strand of beads from the hank and knot the two ends of the strand together to form a circle. You may need to remove a few of the beads so there is enough thread to tie the ends together. Repeat with two more strands.

9 Twist beads

Loop an end of one bead ring around each index finger, then twist the strands together. To keep the strand from untwisting, insert the loop from one finger through the loop on the other finger. Repeat for the other two bead rings.

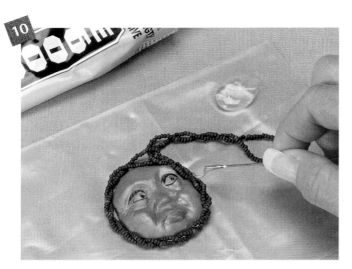

10 Secure face and beads to plastic surface

Squeeze a bit of industrial-strength glue, like E-6000 glue, onto the back of the clay face, then press it onto a plastic sandwich bag. Apply a small amount of glue along the edge of the face, some on the clay and some on the plastic. Position the twisted beads around the face. Use a needle tool to apply more glue if needed. Lightly press the beads into the glue to secure them to the sides of the face and to the plastic. Glue on another ring of twisted beads to frame the face.

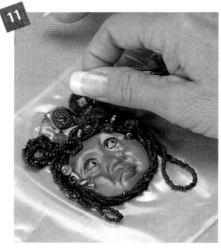

11 Create headdress

Add a little more glue above the twisted beads and cluster the last ring of twisted beads above the face to create a headdress. Squeeze some glue right above the headdress, then add beads, coins and other embellishments.

12 Add small beads

Fill in any exposed glue by pouring seed beads over the face.

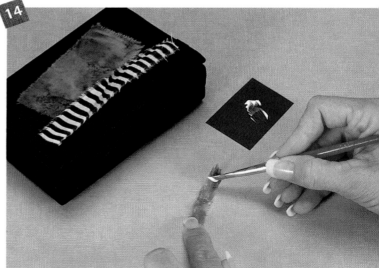

13 Add feather

Use the needle tool to add a touch of glue to the top of the headdress, then tuck a feather into the glue. Pour off any excess seed beads and set the face aside to dry overnight.

14 Decorate purse with fabric

Select fabric for embellishments, then rip the fabric into strips of various sizes. Arrange the pieces on the front of the purse in a pleasing arrangement. Brush washable fabric glue onto the backs of the fabric strips and attach them to the purse. Let the glue dry.

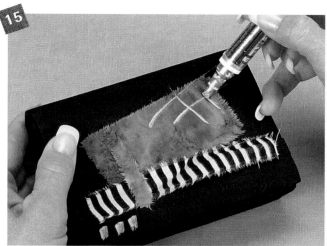

15 Add gold accents
Use a gold leafing pen to add accents across the fabric.

16 Glue face on purse
Peel off the plastic backing from the clay face. Apply fabric glue to the back of the clay face and surrounding headdress, then press the piece onto the purse. Allow the glue to dry completely.

*Finished Purse

You'll turn heads when you carry this purse. Push molds come in a wide variety of shapes—next time try a cat, a flower, a tree or a heart. Browse the aisles of your craft store's clay section for inspiration.

*MORE FUN Art to Wear

If you enjoyed working with polymer clay, keep going! Use a slightly smaller face push mold to make these sunny brooches.

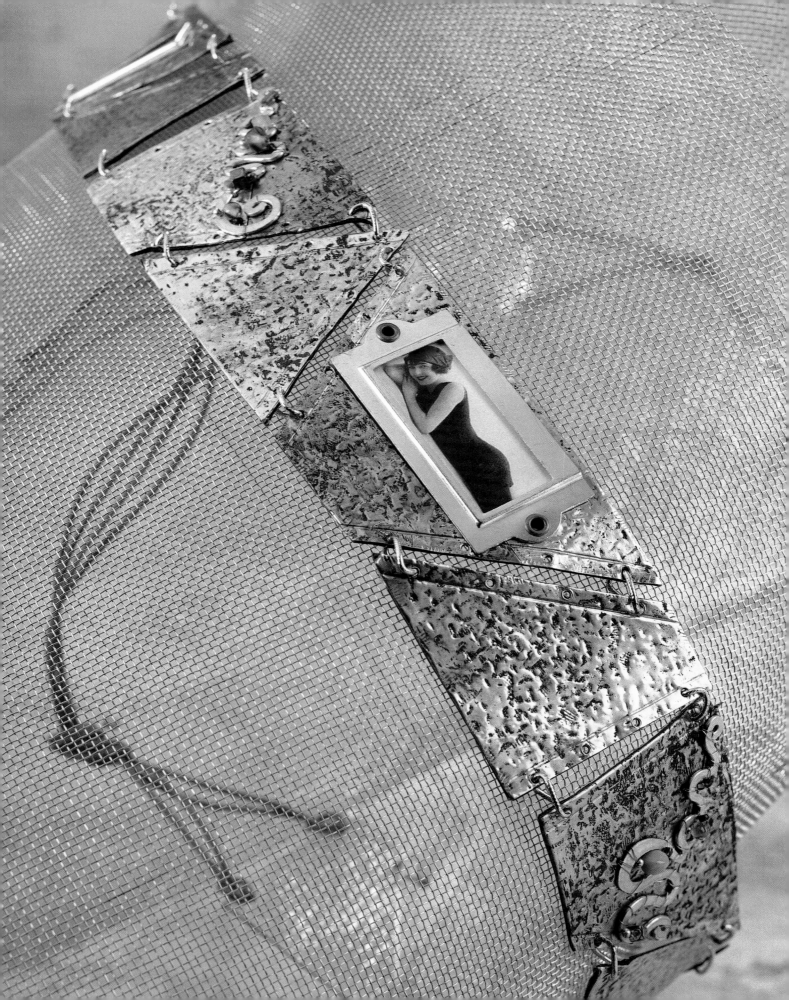

This belt is a great way to express your creativity by experimenting with color and texture as you transform brass, copper and aluminum metal sheets into an exotic work of wearable art. This is a longer project, but don't let the number of steps intimidate you. Once you've completed the first few steps, you'll find that the process is really quite easy—and fun.

Metal Patchwork Belt

MATERIALS AND TOOLS

patchwork template
SEE PAGE 64

sheet of brass embossing metal

sheet of copper embossing metal

sheet of aluminum embossing metal

sheet of peel-and-stick double-sided tape

metal 8 mesh screen

brown ink pad, like Stazon Timber Brown

rust ink pad, like Metal Stamp Art

black acrylic paint

black cardstock

assorted amber beads

antique brass eyelets

4 gold bookplates,
2 small, 2 medium

vintage images, like #M111 Mini Chix,
from ARTchix Studio
AVAILABLE AT CRAFT AND/OR SCRAPBOOKING STORES

36" (91cm) of ¹⁄₁₆" (2mm) silver armature wire

72" (183cm) of 32-gauge brass beading wire

4 yards (4m) of light brown leather cord

gold jump rings

textured rubber mallet
SEE BASIC SUPPLIES, PAGE 9

craft foam sheet

heat gun

brayer

cutting mat

rotary cutter

needle tool

industrial-strength adhesive or
glue made for metal, like E-6000

craft glue

eyelet setter and punch set

hammer

¹⁄₁₆" (2mm) hole punch

¹⁄₈" (3mm) hole punch

wire cutters

round-nose jewelry pliers

fine-tip permanent marker

sheet of paper

pencil

paper towels

ruler

scissors

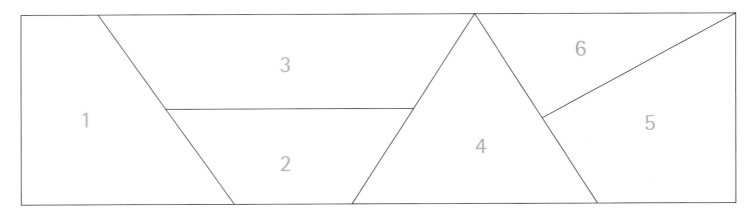

COPY THIS TEMPLATE AND USE IT TO CUT YOUR METAL STRIPS INTO THE APPROPRIATE SIZES AND SHAPES (SEE STEPS 1 AND 10, PAGES 64 AND 66). THE TEMPLATE IS SHOWN AT FULL SIZE.

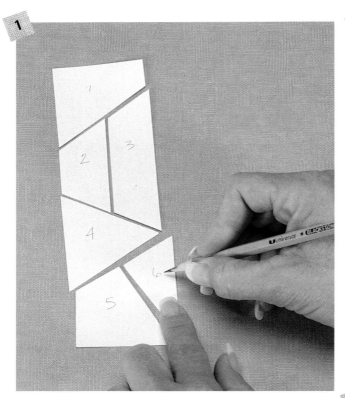

2 Cut metal strips

On a cutting mat, use a rotary cutter to cut ten 7" x 2" (18cm x 5cm) strips from the metal embossing sheets, four from the aluminum, three from the copper and three from the brass.

1 Create patchwork pattern

Photocopy the patchwork template. Cut out the pattern along the perimeter, then cut along the interior lines to divide the pattern into several numbered pieces. These numbered "patches" will serve as the pattern for your belt.

3 Cut double-sided tape

Use a rotary cutter to cut six 7" x 2" (18cm x 5cm) strips from a sheet of peel-and-stick double-sided tape, placed logo side down and shiny side up on the cutting mat to keep them from slipping.

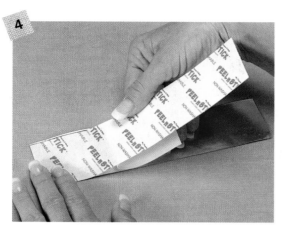

4 Apply tape to metal strips

Peel the backing off of one strip of double-sided tape and apply it to one strip of metal, aligning the edges. Repeat with the five remaining metal strips. In total, you should apply the double-sided tape to two aluminum strips, two brass strips and two copper strips.

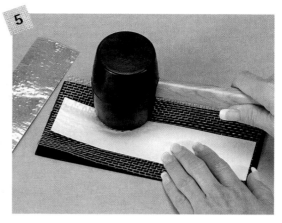

5 Texture metal

Place a piece of metal 8 mesh screen onto a sheet of craft foam to cushion it. Place one of the metal strips with the tape adhered, metal side down, on top of the screen and hammer it with a textured rubber mallet (see Basic Techniques, page 12). Repeat with the five remaining metal strips backed with double-sided tape.

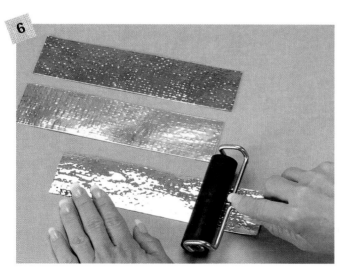

6 Flatten metal

Remove the metal strips from the screen and craft foam and run a brayer over each one of them (metal side up) to flatten them. You may want to experiment with different mesh counts to find the one you like best.

7 Antique metal

Lay two metal strips at a time on a scrap piece of paper, then ink the metal by rubbing a brown ink pad against the surface of the metal. Follow by inking with the rust ink pad in the same fashion while the brown ink is still wet. Use paper towels to blot off any areas that you feel have too much ink.

8 Heat set ink

Heat the metal with a heat gun for about 30 seconds to set the ink, keeping the gun moving continually over the ink until it is dry. (If excess ink appears to rest on the surface of the metal, gently dab it off with a paper towel.)

9 Add black paint

Squeeze a line of black acrylic paint onto each metal strip and use a paper towel to rub it into the textured surface. Wipe off any excess paint. If the paint begins to dry before you are satisfied with the result, dampen the surface slightly with water and resume rubbing.

10 Mark and cut metal strips

Place the paper pattern pieces over one metal strip in the order indicated by the numbers and align the edges. Score the metal along the edges of each pattern piece with a stylus or pencil, and then cut the score lines with scissors. Repeat with the five remaining strips until they are all cut into patches.

11 Lay out four patchwork strips

Since you cut apart six strips of metal using the same pattern, you should have six identically sized metal pieces for every pattern segment. Use the paper pattern as your guide to lay out the metal pieces into four strips, mixing the different-colored metal patches on each strip to create a patchwork effect. You will only use four completed patchwork strips for the belt. The other pieces can be used to make a matching accessory.

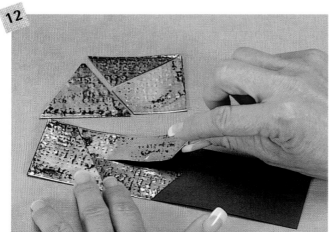

12 Adhere patches to cardstock strips

Cut four 7" x 2" (18cm x 5cm) strips of black cardstock. Working piece by piece from the reassembled strips, peel the backings off of the tape on the backs of the metal patches and adhere the patches in order to the cardstock strip. Attach the patches to all four strips of cardstock.

13 Back strips with metal

Cut four more 7" x 2" (18cm x 5cm) strips from the double-sided tape sheet. Adhere the tape to the back of each cardstock strip and peel off the backing. Adhere the four remaining metal strips from step two to the backs of the patchwork strips. You should now have four patchwork metal strips, each backed with metal. Trim any edges that are not in alignment.

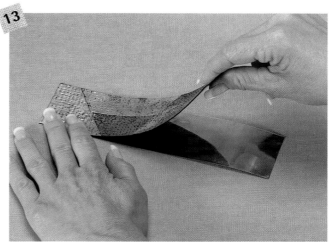

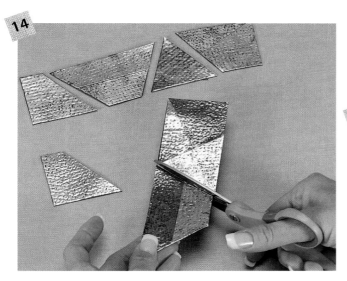

14 Cut apart patchwork strips

Cut each patchwork strip into four pieces to create two pieces that are solid-colored and two pieces that are double-colored. Using the numbered template as a guide, each strip will be cut into four separate pieces: 1, 2 and 3, 4, 5 and 6 (according to the template).

15 Make scrolled accents

Use round-nose jewelry pliers to bend and curl four 8" (20cm) pieces of armature wire into scrolls. Each one should be slightly different. With a hammer, flatten each scroll (see Basic Techniques, pages 12–13). Check the size of each piece against the template after hammering and trim with wire cutters if necessary.

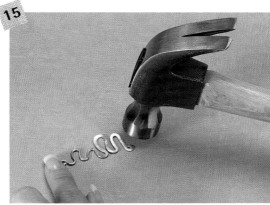

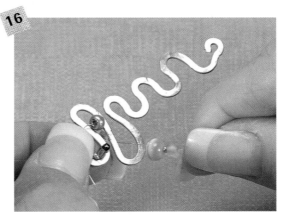

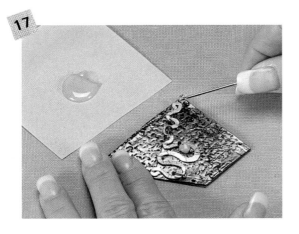

16 Add beads to scrolled accents

String ten to twelve assorted amber beads onto an 18" (46cm) length of 32-gauge brass beading wire. Wrap the wire around a scrolled accent, fastening the bead embellishments to the scroll. Knot the end of the wire to secure it to the scroll. Repeat for the three remaining accents.

17 Secure scrolled and beaded accents

With industrial-strength glue, secure a scrolled and beaded accent piece to one of the end pieces of each metal strip (pieces 5 and 6 according to pattern numbers). Use the needle tool to pick up glue and add it under the accent. Repeat for the other three end pieces.

18 Add gold bookplates

Select two small and two medium gold book-plates. Position one on each of four of the double-colored patches and use a permanent marker to mark the hole placement for each plate. Vary the orientation, placing the plates both vertically and horizontally.

19 Punch holes

Pound the head of the punch from the eyelet setter and punch set with a hammer to make holes as marked on each patch.

20 Set bookplates with eyelets

With the right side of the metal piece facing up, align the bookplate's holes with the holes you punched. Slide eyelets through the aligned holes. Then turn the piece over and pound the head of the eyelet setter punch with a hammer to set the eyelets from the back. Repeat for the three remaining bookplates.

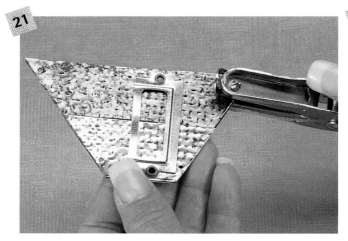

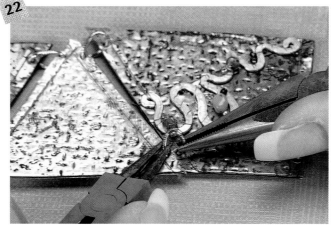

21 Make holes for jump rings

Measure and mark the placement for each jump ring hole. The holes should be consistently placed ¼" (6mm) from the top and the bottom edges on the right and left sides of each piece. At each mark, punch the holes with a ¹⁄₁₆" (2mm) single hole punch. At either end of the belt, punch the metal with a ⅛" (3mm) hole punch.

21 Fasten metal patches together with jump rings

Lay out the patchwork pieces in the order in which you are connecting them. Open two jump rings using round-nose jewelry pliers, then insert the jump rings through the holes on the first piece you are connecting. Attach the next metal patch onto the jump rings, then close the jump rings. Continue fastening the metal patches together until you have completed the entire belt.

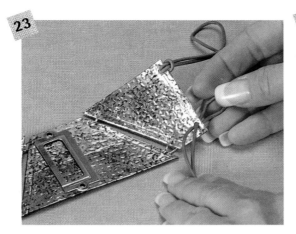

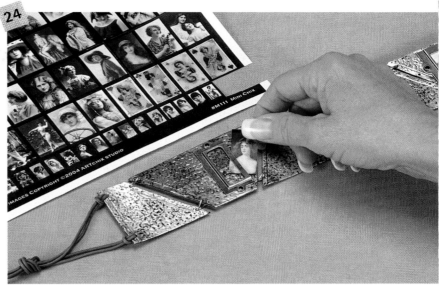

23 Add leather cord

Cut four 36" (91cm) lengths of leather cord. Fold one length in half and lace the folded portion through one of the ⅛" (3mm) holes at the ends of the belt. Secure the leather cord with a lark's head knot as shown above. Repeat with the other three cords. Knot all four strands together as pictured in step 24.

24 Add images to bookplates

Slide a vintage image into each bookplate on the belt. (You may have to crop the image slightly for it to fit neatly into the bookplate.) Adhere each image with craft glue.

*Finished Belt

Pair this belt with your favorite pair of jeans or even with a solid-colored dress for an edgy look. For a softer look, you could even pick just one or two metals to use for the entire belt—for example, aluminum alone or copper and brass.

*MORE FUN
Art to Wear

Use the extra pieces of metal from this project to create one of these fun accessories. Metal adds a new dimension to any object.

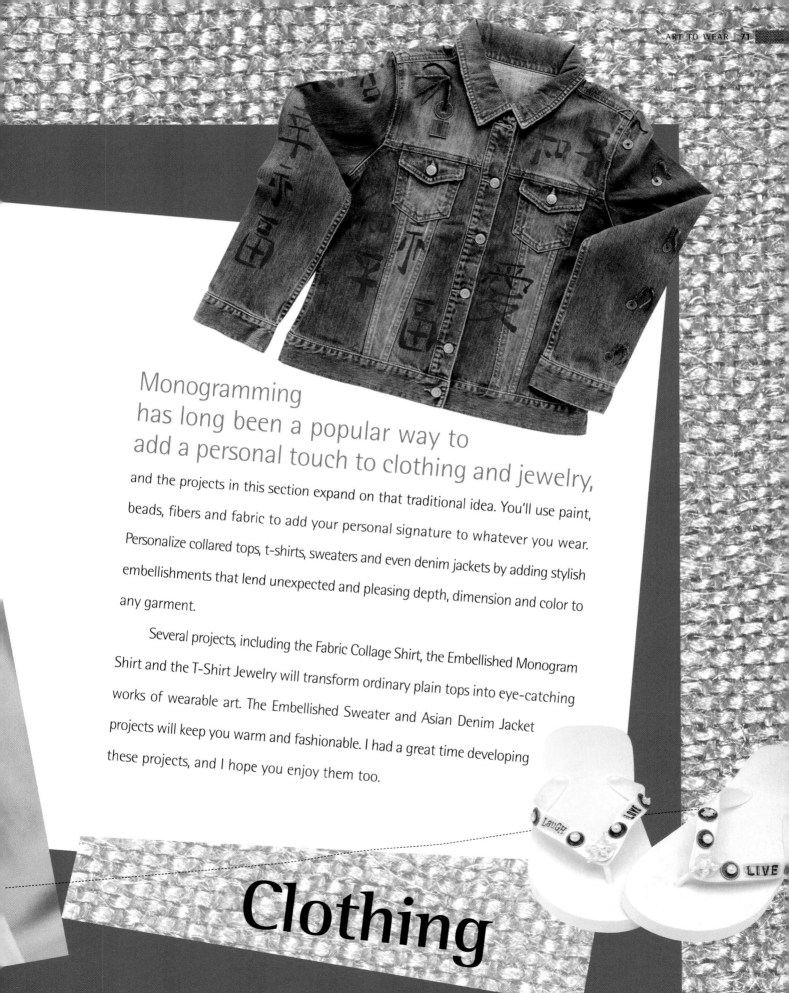

Monogramming
has long been a popular way to
add a personal touch to clothing and jewelry,
and the projects in this section expand on that traditional idea. You'll use paint, beads, fibers and fabric to add your personal signature to whatever you wear. Personalize collared tops, t-shirts, sweaters and even denim jackets by adding stylish embellishments that lend unexpected and pleasing depth, dimension and color to any garment.

Several projects, including the Fabric Collage Shirt, the Embellished Monogram Shirt and the T-Shirt Jewelry will transform ordinary plain tops into eye-catching works of wearable art. The Embellished Sweater and Asian Denim Jacket projects will keep you warm and fashionable. I had a great time developing these projects, and I hope you enjoy them too.

Clothing

What comes first, the fabric collage or the shirt? When my mother and I were working on this project, we started with the fabric collage. We found that each process led naturally to the next, from initial concept and fabric selection to surface design, stitching, gluing and embellishing. Then we had a great time taking the finished piece with us as we shopped for the perfect garment to embellish with it.

Fabric Collage Shirt

MATERIALS AND TOOLS

front-button shirt, in a
material like linen or cotton

various swatches of fabric in different colors
and patterns that coordinate with the shirt
ONE SWATCH SHOULD BE BIG ENOUGH TO BE
THE BACKGROUND FOR THE COLLAGE

dimensional decorative objects, such as fabric
cord and dimensional scrapbooking words

fabric image, like the
ones from ARTchix Studio

heat-bond fusible webbing
AVAILABLE AT FABRIC AND CRAFT STORES

sewing machine and thread
OPTIONAL

iron
TACKING OR REGULAR

washable fabric glue

1 Select and cut out collage elements

Choose the fabrics and components, including cord, images and text, that you would like to use for the collage. The materials can be a combination of colors, patterns and textures. Decide on the size of the design, taking into consideration the size of the garment. Cut out or tear out the collage elements.

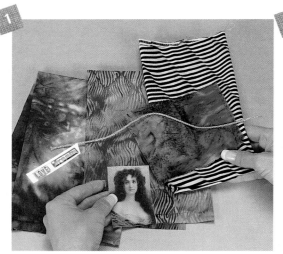

Tip* *There's no reason to be intimidated by the sewing machine. Just think back to your home ec training and make a few practice runs before you begin to sew your project.*

For simple straight stitching, set the stitch width at 0 and the stitch length at 3 or 4. Place your project in the machine, drop the presser foot and sew a straight seam. Stop and make turns where needed. Lift the presser foot, trim the thread and remove the project when finished.

2 Compose collage

Place the collage elements on a fabric backing to make a pleasing composition. Once you have decided on your composition, use washable fabric glue to secure the elements to the fabric backing. For a collaged look, don't be afraid to overlap, lift and tuck as you are gluing.

3 Add decorative stitching

Use a sewing machine to stitch down and around random elements. Because this step is decorative, you can pick and choose which elements you want to accent with stitching. Or, if you'd like, you can omit this step; just make sure all of the collage elements are secured with glue.

4 Apply additional elements

Glue on any additional dimensional elements, such as cord and dimensional words. Even if the words are self-adhesive, use washable glue to secure the bond.

5 Iron on fusible webbing

Cut a piece of heat-bond fusible webbing slightly smaller than the fabric backing. Place the collage face down on your work surface, then place the fusible webbing, shiny side down, on the back of the fabric. Use an iron at medium-high heat to adhere the webbing to the fabric. Press firmly with the iron for 15-second intervals, continuing until the webbing is secure.

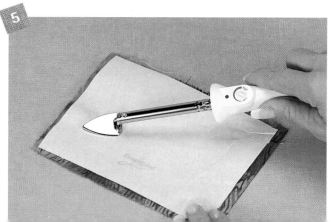

6 Remove backing from fusible webbing

Peel away the paper backing from the fusible webbing.

7 Iron collage onto shirt

Position the fabric collage as desired on the shirt, then run a medium-high iron over the collage to secure it. Again, press firmly with the iron for 15-second intervals, continuing until the collage is secure. Use caution to avoid scorching your collage. Do not iron over dimensional words.

*Finished Fabric Collage

This one-of-a-kind shirt bears the stamp of your personality. Pair it with slacks or a casual skirt to complete a look that's all you. Always hand wash your wearable art garments.

*MORE FUN Art to Wear

Design a fabric collage to make an original purse or tote. In addition to using fusible webbing, you can adhere fabric collages to almost any surface using glue, stitching or double-sided tape.

White on white has a soft yet interesting look that is always appealing, and this monogrammed t-shirt with just the right amount of beaded embellishments has a very classic feel. I made this shirt for my sister Lisa, so the design came together with her in mind. It's always more fun to design a piece with someone specific in mind—you find yourself matching the elements you use to the wearer's personality traits.

Embellished
Monogram T-Shirt

MATERIALS AND TOOLS

clean t-shirt
WHITE

iron-on washable, dyeable monogram
WHITE

embellishments, such as faux pearls,
Chinese coins, buttons with thread
through the holes, gold spacer beads
and white frosted E-beads

dimensional scrapbooking words

size 11 seed beads

36" (91cm) beading thread
WHITE

beading needle

iron
TACKING OR REGULAR

washable fabric glue

1/16" (2mm) hole punch

scissors

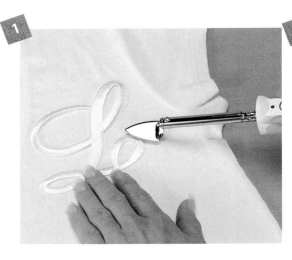

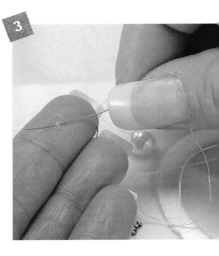

1 Iron monogram onto shirt

Position the monogram on the upper-right part of the shirt as desired. Iron the monogram onto the shirt, setting the iron according to the care label of the garment. Press firmly with the iron for 15-second intervals, continuing until the monogram is secure. Use caution to avoid scorching the monogram.

2 Glue on design elements

Lay out the larger design elements that might be difficult to sew, like the Chinese coins and the threaded buttons, onto the shirt around the monogram to create a pleasing composition. Glue them on with washable fabric glue. The rest of the elements (beads and dimensional word) will be sewed onto the shirt.

3 Stitch on beads

Thread your beading needle with a 24" to 36" (61cm to 91cm) length of white beading thread. Knot the end of the thread. Stitching from inside the shirt, pull the needle through to the front in the spot where the pearl or other "base" bead is to be attached. String the bead onto the needle and slide the bead down the thread to the surface of the shirt. Slide a seed bead onto your thread.

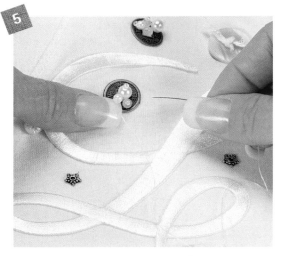

4 Make and secure bead clusters

Rest the seed bead on top of the pearl (or other base bead). Pass the needle back through the bottom bead and through to the inside of the shirt. Knot the thread on the inside of the shirt to secure the beads. Use the same technique to make and secure multiple beads (bead clusters).

5 Add bead clusters to coins

Using the techniques from steps 3 and 4, stitch a bead cluster onto the center of each Chinese coin.

6 Add gold spacer beads

Using the techniques from steps 3 and 4, secure the spacer beads with their bead clusters of E-beads to the shirt.

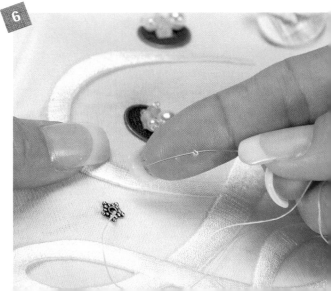

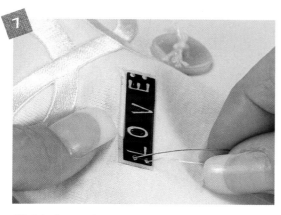

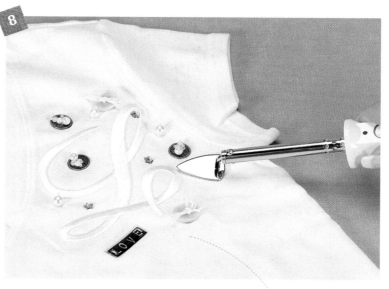

7 Stitch on dimensional word

With a ¹⁄₁₆" (2mm) hole punch, punch two holes on each end of the dimensional scrapbooking word. Place the dimensional word on the shirt as desired, then secure it to the shirt by stitching through the holes.

8 Re-iron monogram

When finished, re-iron the monogram letter, taking care to avoid touching the embellishments with the hot iron.

*Finished T-Shirt

This personalized t-shirt makes a great gift—this design will look perfect on my sister Lisa. You can adjust your embellishing elements to fit the person you're making this t-shirt for, too. Maybe she'd like bright, multi-colored beads or a black-and-silver bead combo. Always hand wash your wearable art garments.

*MORE FUN
Art to Wear

Accessorize your outfit with a matching pair of flip-flops and jewelry set. Stitch the embellishments onto an ordinary pair of flip-flops, then make a necklace and a pair of earrings using some of the jewelry-making techniques described in the first section of this book.

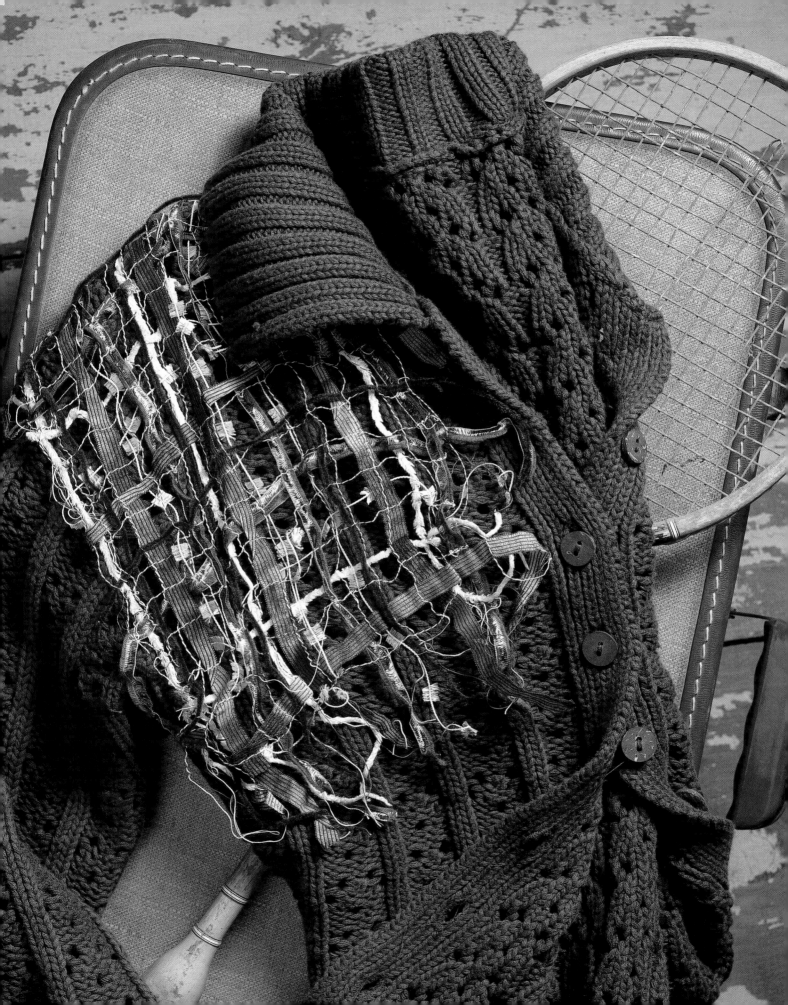

Fibers make a great embellishment for any number of things, and they are the perfect accent for this plain sweater. As I worked on this project, I found that every process was as exciting as the next, and I couldn't wait to see the end results. You'll have a great time working with these beautiful fibers and watching the interesting water-soluble sheets dissolve like magic as you create your design.

Embellished Sweater

MATERIALS AND TOOLS

knitted sweater in a solid color

coordinating fibers, like those
made by Adornaments
AVAILABLE IN PREPACKAGED SETS
AT CRAFT AND FABRIC STORES

scrap of cotton fabric

2 heavy water-soluble
stabilizer sheets, like those
made by Sulky Super Solvy
AVAILABLE IN VARIOUS SIZES AT
CRAFT AND FABRIC STORES

thread in a color to
match sweater and fibers

sewing machine

bowl of water

hand soap or dish soap

towel

needle

iron

scissors

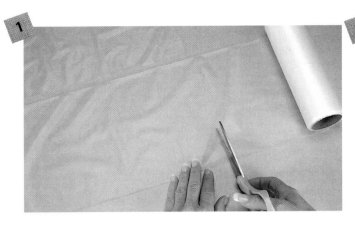

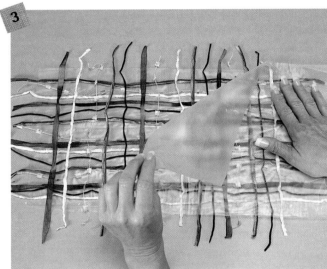

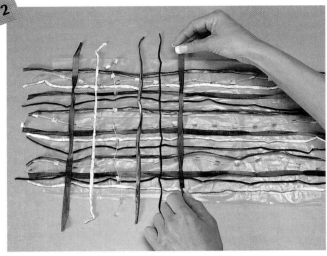

1 Cut stabilizer sheets

Determine the size of your decorative swatch, taking into consideration the sweater (or other garment) to be adorned. Cut two pieces of water-soluble stabilizer sheet to that size and lay out one sheet.

2 Cut fibers and lay out in grid

Select five different kinds of fibers. For a patch approximately 8" x 15" (20cm x 38cm), cut six lengths of each kind of fiber: three 22" (56cm) lengths and three 12" (30cm) lengths. Place the longer lengths horizontally on the stabilizer sheet, spaced ½" (1cm) to 1" (3cm) apart. Place the shorter lengths vertically on top of the horizontal fibers, again ½" (1cm) to 1" (3cm) apart. Do not worry if the layout of the fibers is a bit irregular. The ends of the fibers may dangle off of the stabilizer sheet.

3 Iron stabilizer sheets together

Lay the second stabilizer sheet on top of the fibers, creating a "sandwich." Lay a piece of fabric over the top stabilizer sheet. If not using an ironing board, also lay a piece of fabric underneath the sandwich. Iron the two stabilizer sheets together using medium-high heat. Press firmly with the iron for 15-second intervals, continuing until the sheets are fused together.

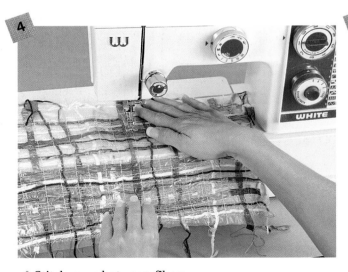

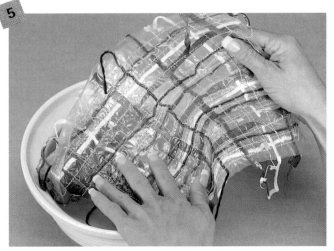

4 Stitch rows between fibers

Use a sewing machine to stitch rows between both the horizontal and vertical fibers. Your stitched rows should be about ½" (1cm) apart. Back stitch at the beginning and end of each row to secure the stitched threads. Trim any long fibers around the edges. Or leave the edges irregular, if you prefer.

5 Dissolve stabilizer sheets

Submerge the fused stabilizer sheets in a bowl of cool water and agitate the water with your hands until you feel the sheets melting into a gel. Continue to rinse the fibers with fresh water until the stabilizer has completely dissolved, rubbing in a bit of hand soap or dish soap to expedite the dissolving process.

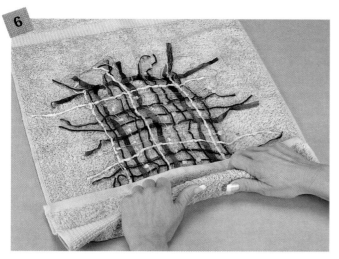

6 Dry fiber swatch

Lay the wet fiber swatch on a towel and roll it up jelly-roll style to rid the fibers of excess water. Unroll the towel and allow the swatch to air dry.

7 Fold swatch, place on sweater

Lay the dry fiber swatch on your work surface. Fold one corner over, over-lapping the swatch in a triangle shape. Position the swatch along one shoulder of the sweater, with the folded edge closest to the collar.

8 Stitch swatch to sweater

Thread a sewing needle with thread to match the sweater and hand stitch the swatch to the front of the sweater. Secure the swatch with stitches in about four different places. Finish by stitching the swatch to the back of the sweater, again securing with stitches in about four different places.

*Finished Sweater

The fiber swatch adds interesting color and texture to the sweater, highlighting the rich brown yarn and the eyelet stitch. Try this technique with any solid-colored sweater. Always hand wash your wearable art garments.

*MORE FUN
Art to Wear

Take the technique you learned from this sweater project to make a fashionable scarf using your choice of fibers. For an extra touch, you can finish the scarf by tying beads onto the fringed ends.

I call this piece T-Shirt Jewelry because, well, it's a t-shirt that's "wearing" a necklace. This spunky t-shirt was another Mom-and-me project. We've dressed up this tank top using handmade fabric beads and funky fibers. Using scraps of hand-dyed fabrics, metallic threads and fibers, we glued and wrapped these colorful little beads while we enjoyed each other's company. This is a great project to share with someone special.

T-Shirt Jewelry

MATERIALS AND TOOLS

tank top or scoop neck shirt
(I USED WHITE)

plastic drinking straws

swatch of decorative fabric

metallic thread

scrap of craft wire

decorative thread or fibers

4 silver jump rings

2 spring clasps

thread to match shirt color

flat paintbrush

needle

washable fabric glue

needle-nose pliers

scissors

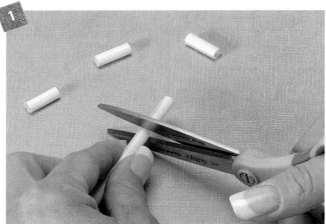

1 Cut straws

Use scissors to cut the straws into twelve 1" (3cm) pieces.

2 Cut fabric squares

Tear the decorative fabric into 1" (3cm) wide strips, then cut the strips into 1" (3cm) square pieces. When tearing fabric, it helps to make a small cut at the edge of the fabric to start the tear.

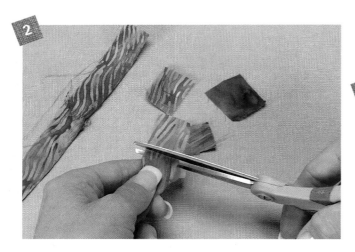

3 Glue fabric to straws

Brush washable glue onto the back of a fabric square, then wrap the square around a straw segment to cover it. Repeat with the remaining straw segments and fabric squares.

4 Wrap with metallic thread

Wrap metallic thread around the center of each fabric-covered straw segment about fifteen to twenty times. On the final wrap, knot the two ends of thread together. Trim the threads, leaving a small tail.

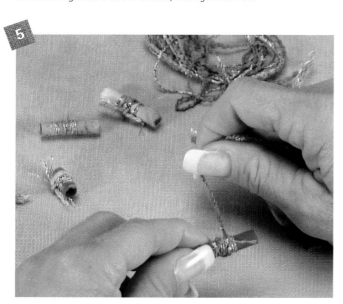

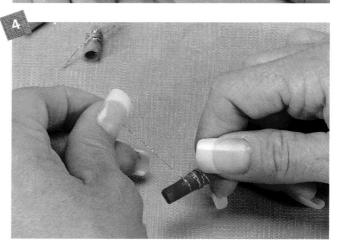

5 Wrap with decorative thread

Wrap decorative thread over the metallic thread twice. After the second wrap, knot the two ends of thread together. Trim the threads, leaving a small tail.

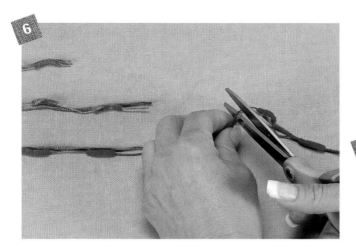

6 Cut decorative thread

Cut one length of decorative thread to 17" (43cm), another length to 19" (48cm) and a third length to 21" (53cm).

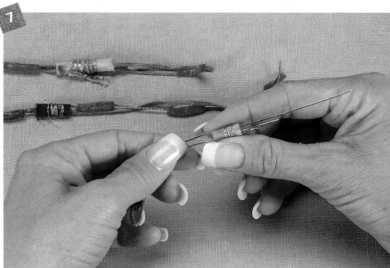

7 String beads

String four fabric-wrapped beads onto each length of decorative thread. Check out the tip on this page to learn an easy way to string beads using a small piece of craft wire.

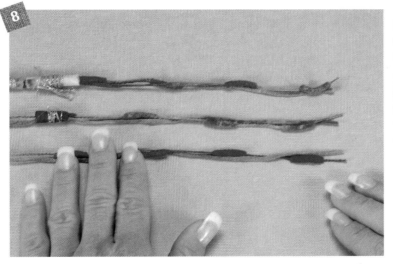

Tip* *An easy way to string beads onto thread is to make and use your own "needle." Fold a piece of craft wire in half and place the thread inside the fold. Then, slip the beads over the wire and directly onto the thread.*

8 Line up beaded decorative thread

Line up the three lengths of beaded decorative thread so that all of the ends are even on one side.

9 Knot ends

Tie the three even ends of thread in a single knot.

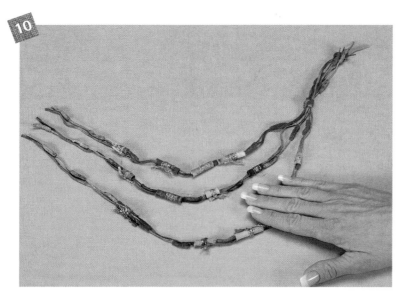

10 Arrange threads and tie ends

Lay out the beaded threads and make the three remaining ends meet, arranging the threads in the form of a cascading necklace. Tie the ends of the three threads in a knot.

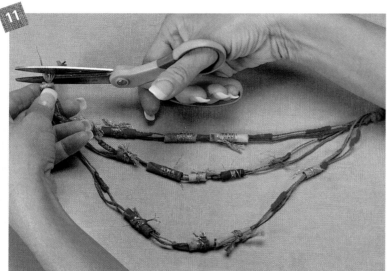

11 Trim end fringes

Trim the fringes from the end of each knot.

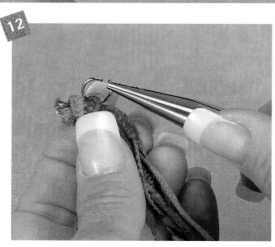

12 Attach jump ring

Open a silver jump ring with needle-nose pliers, then catch a few strands of the knotted threads inside the ring. Repeat on the other side.

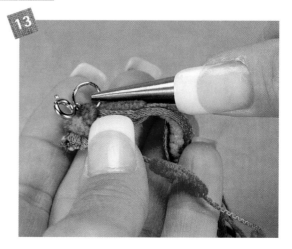

13 Attach spring clasp

Attach a spring clasp to the jump ring, then close the jump ring to secure the clasp. Repeat to add a spring clasp to the other jump ring.

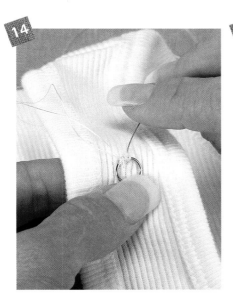

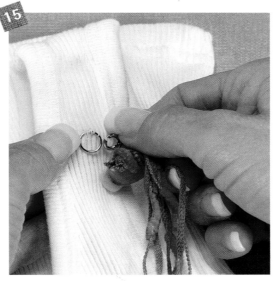

14 Sew jump ring onto shirt

Using a needle and thread, sew two jump rings onto the shirt, one just below each shoulder.

15 Attach "necklace" to shirt

Secure each end of the "necklace" to the shirt by attaching each spring clasp to each jump ring on the shirt.

*Finished Tank Top

With the built-in jewelry on this top, you won't even need to wear a necklace. This tank will look good with shorts or jeans—maybe even the pair with Pocket Jewelry. Detach the necklace before washing the tank top.

*MORE FUN
Art to Wear

Use the fabric- and thread-wrapped beads to make a "necklace" to wrap around the brim of your favorite hat.

Denim jackets are something most people have in their closets, and they make great canvases for your artwork. This project shows you how to jazz up a denim jacket with a simple stencil design, some studs and a few dangling coins. The beautiful Asian motif puts a sophisticated spin on a piece of clothing that you might otherwise take for granted.

Asian Denim Jacket

MATERIALS AND TOOLS

denim jacket

acrylic paints in varying shades of blue,
like Wedgewood Blue, Uniform Blue and
Williamsburg Blue from DecoArt Americana

Chinese character stencils,
like "Peace, Love, Happiness,"
by Yasutomo
AVAILABLE AT CRAFT STORES

decorative studs

decorative blue fiber thread,
two different styles

20 small Chinese coins, approximately
½" (1cm) in diameter

1 large Chinese coin, approximately
1¼" (3cm) in diameter

stud setter

stencil brush

thin-tipped black
permanent marker

crochet hook

craft knife

scissors

ruler

1 Stencil jacket front and sleeve

Stencil the Chinese characters, placing them as desired on the front of the jacket and down one sleeve. Apply the darkest blue with a stencil brush first, followed immediately by a light application of the lightest blue as a highlight. Blend the colors on the fabric. There is no need to let the first application of paint dry before adding the highlights.

2 Stencil jacket back

After the front of the jacket has dried, stencil the same characters onto the back of the denim jacket, placing the three characters in a vertical column down the center. If your stencil includes a translation of the character, stencil the word below each character, as shown.

3 Place and set studs

Place decorative studs about 1" (3cm) apart along the horizontal seam on the jacket back. Firmly press each stud into the seam, then place the stud setter directly over each stud. Press down on the handle of the setter to secure each stud. When the back is done, set studs along the seam above the pockets on the jacket front.

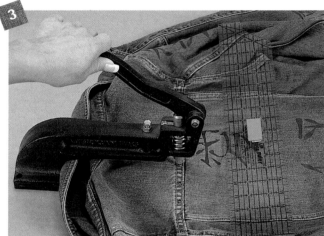

4 Knot thread through small coins

Cut six to ten 8" (20cm) lengths of each kind of blue thread. Fold one thread in half and loop it onto the crochet hook. Pull the thread through the opening of a small Chinese coin. When the thread is through the opening, make a lark's head knot to secure the coin. Repeat for the remaining coins, alternating between fibers for each coin.

5 Mark and cut sleeves

Starting from the top of the unpainted sleeve and working toward the cuff, use a thin-tipped permanent marker to mark the denim with one set of two dots about ⅛" (3mm) apart. Continue marking the sleeve with sets of dots every 4" (10cm) until you reach the cuff. Use the tip of a craft knife to cut a small hole through each dot.

7 Secure coins to jacket back

Repeating the techniques from steps 5 and 6, secure coins on the jacket back by guiding the thread through sets of vertical holes placed about 2½" (6cm) apart. The coins should be tied in a row just below the double-stitched seam.

6 Secure Chinese coins to sleeve

Thread both tails of the knotted Chinese coin threads onto a crochet hook, then guide the hook through one hole and then back out the other. Knot the two tails together to secure the coin to the denim. When knotted, the knot and two tails will emerge from one hole and the coin will emerge from the other. Repeat for each set of holes, keeping the tail side and the coin side consistent as you work down the sleeve. Trim off any excessively long threads to make them all uniform.

*Finished Jacket

With its up-to-the-minute style, this jacket can be a great accent to any outfit. Your friends will be asking you where they can buy one for themselves. Always hand wash your wearable art garments.

8 Add large coin to jacket

Cut one 8" (20cm) length of each kind of blue fiber thread. As in step 4, use a crochet hook to pull both threads through the opening of the large Chinese coin and secure it with a lark's head knot. Using the techniques from steps 5, 6 and 7, secure the large coin above one of the front pockets, close to the collar.

*MORE FUN Art to Wear

Use some of the left over Chinese coins and the jewelry-making techniques from the first section of this book to make earrings that match your jacket.

Resources

All of the materials used in the projects in this book can be purchased at your local craft, fabric, scrapbooking and rubber-stamping stores or at discount department stores. If you are unable to find what you need at a local store, contact the manufacturers listed below for a retailer near you.

AMACO (American Art Clay Co., Inc.)
6060 Guion Rd.
Indianapolis, IN 46254
(800) 374-1600
www.amaco.com
* FIMO Soft polymer clay, Faces Push Mold, Patina Rub 'n Buff, embossing metals

American Tag Co.
2043 Saybrook Ave.
Commerce, CA 90040
(800) 223-3956
www.americantag.net
* studs, stud setter

ARTchix Studio
585 Stornoway Dr.
Victoria, BC
V9C3L1 Canada
www.artchixstudio.com
* paper and fabric vintage images

DecoArt
P.O. Box 386
Stanford, KY 40484
(606) 365-3193
www.decoart.com
* Americana acrylic paints

EK Success Ltd.
125 Entin Rd.
Clifton, NJ 07014
(800) 524-1349
www.eksuccess.com
* Adornments fibers, letter stickers

Fiskars Brands, Inc.
7811 W. Stewart Ave.
Wausau, WI 54401
(800) 500-4849
www.fiskars.com
* hole punch, wire cutters, rotary cutter

Hirschberg Schultz & Co.
650 Liberty Ave.
Union, NJ 07083
(908) 810-1111
* memory wire, ear wires

Jacquard Products/Rupert Gibbon & Spider, Inc.
P.O. Box 425
Healdsburg, CA 95448
(707) 433-9577
www.jacquardproducts.com
* Piñata inks, Pearl Ex powdered pigments

Jo-Ann Scrap Essentials
Hudson, OH 44233
* metal book plates

Krylon
101 Prospect Ave. NW 1500 Midland Bldg.
Cleveland, OH 44115
(216) 515-7693
www.krylon.com
* gold leafing pen

Pepperell Braiding Co.
P.O. Box 1487
Pepperell, MA 01463
(800) 343-8114
www.pepperell.com
* clear tubing, leather cording

Plaid Enterprises, Inc.
3225 Westech Dr.
Norcross, GA 30092
(678) 291-8100
www.plaidonline.com
* découpage medium, paintbrushes, stencils

Stanislaus Imports Inc.
41 14th St.
San Francisco, CA 94103
(415) 431-7122
www.stanislausimports.com
* mini game pieces, Chinese coins

Sulky of America Inc.
3113 Broadpoint Dr.
Harbor Heights, FL 33983
(941) 629-3199
www.sulky.com
* Super Solvy

Tape Systems, Inc.
460 East Sandford Blvd.
Mount Vernon, NY 10550
(914) 668-3700
www.tapesys.com
* miscellaneous supplies

The Warm Company
954 East Union St.
Seattle, WA 98122
(800) 234-warm
www.warmcompany.com
* fusible webbing

Tsukineko, Inc.
17640 NE 65th St.
Redmond, WA 98052
(425) 883-7733
www.tsukineko.com
* StazOn inkpad

Uchida of America Corp.
3535 Del Amo Blvd.
Torrance, CA 90503
(310) 869-6388
www.uchida.com
* heat gun

Yasutomo
490 Eccles Ave.
So. San Francisco, CA 94080
(650) 737-8888
www.yasutomo.com
* Chinese character stencils